D0944215

TO FORT SMITH

◆ OTHER TOWNS
● OTHER TOWNS
× OTHER PLACES
MENTIONED IN TEXT.
++++++++ STATE LINES
-------- COUNTY LINES

Floyd W. Pratt

kchi'

Mc

sboro

CURTAIN

Little River

Pecan
Point

Idabel

Pecan Bayou

Clarksville

ARKANSAS

Red River

Fulton

BOWIE

Boston

Texarkana

MILLER

RIVER

River

US

TO
SHREVEPORT

THE RED RIVER VALLEY
THEN AND NOW

Christmas
'48

To

The family Pratt

with

accent on Floyd.

Floyd and Lucile

THE
RED RIVER VALLEY
THEN AND NOW

BY

A. W. NEVILLE

STORIES *of* PEOPLE *and* EVENTS
*In the Red River Valley During the First
Hundred Years of Its Settlement*

ILLUSTRATED *by* JOSÉ CISNEROS

PARIS : TEXAS : 1948

DESIGNED AND PRODUCED BY
CARL HERTZOG : EL PASO, TEXAS

COPYRIGHT 1948
NORTH TEXAS PUBLISHING COMPANY : PARIS, TEXAS

To

A. G. MAYSE

and

HOUSTON HARTE

One suggested these stories
as a newspaper feature;
the other asked they be
preserved in a book.
Here it is.

HOW TO READ THE STORIES

THESE STORIES *should not be read as history. Some have dates, others do not, and history must have dates and footnotes to cite authority.*

They should not be read as biography; though men and women are named in them, it is not in a biographical sense, but to connect them with the incidents. The purpose of the stories is to give the reader some knowledge of the first hundred years of the settlement of the Valley—of the people and some of the things they did or that were done to them.

I have lived in the Valley near seventy years. The stories come from personal experience, from court records and government archives, from contemporary newspapers, from people who told them to me. They are not chronological, and each is complete in itself.

Largely they are of life "in the raw," because life was much like that during a great part of the first hundred years. That it is not so today is because we are no longer pioneers, but are fast becoming numbers on a filing card and have not the stomach for achieving our own security, as did the men and women who came into the Valley and made it support them by plowing the soil to produce food, felling the forests for home building, and making it a Valley fit for coming generations. If the stories awaken in even one individual a determination to rely on himself, and to stand or fall by his own effort, I shall feel that I have not written in vain.

A. W. NEVILLE

Paris, Texas, July 4, 1948

[vii]

CONTENTS

THE VALLEY—THEN AND NOW

From San Augustine, Texas, January 9, 1836, David Crockett wrote to his children in Tennessee: "I must say as to what I have seen of Texas it is the garden spot of the world, the best land and the best prospects for health I ever saw is here . . . I expect in all probability to settle on Bodark or Choctaw Bayou of Red River, that I have no doubt is the richest country in the world, good land and plenty of timber, and the best springs and good mill streams, good range, clear water and every appearance of health. Game a plenty. It is in the pass where the buffalo passes from north to south and back twice a year, and bees and honey plenty.

"I have great hopes of getting the agency to settle that country . . . I have but little doubt of being elected a member to form a constitution for this province . . . I am rejoiced at my fate. I had rather be in my present position than to be elected to a seat in Congress for life."

That was the Red River Valley of the time Crockett wrote —that is the Valley of today, though the buffalo do not pass from north to south and back, the power of the mill streams has been replaced by electric current, and while bees and honey are plenty they are not wild as Crockett found them.

That portion of the Valley, 150 miles long and thirty or more miles wide, reaching from Denison to Texarkana, includes eight counties in Texas and Oklahoma and one in Arkansas, and covers six million acres of land over which Indians once traveled, sometimes at peace with the pioneer settlers, sometimes stealing, sometimes killing and scalping men, women, and children—a Valley red in fact as well as in name.

The stories told in this volume had their beginning more than a century ago, and during the following one hundred years there was in this Valley drama, tragedy and comedy. People lived and loved and hated, were born and did their allotted tasks and died, just as people do today, though in many instances with stouter hearts and more resourcefulness than characterizes the people of today. The stories are not history, though the most of them may be verified from records, should one choose to make search as I have done. Some are without dates, some without names of people, but all have some interest, because they are real life stories.

The river which flows through this Valley — the Rio Roxo of the Spaniards, the Bogue Humma of the Choctaw Indians, the Red River of the Anglo-Saxons who settled the Valley — is different from other rivers forming the boundary between two states, for instead of the middle of the stream being the boundary it lies wholly within the State of Oklahoma where it flows between the two states, the treaty between Spain and United States describing the south cut bank of the river as the boundary.

Red River is notionate, too. In time of flood — and there have been some real floods — it often deserts its channel and chooses another, cutting away the earth and going where it wills, destroying crops and the land on which they grew. But the river is beneficent. It has deposited on its bottoms some of the richest soil on earth, in which everything needed for food for man or beast grows luxuriantly. Early comers to this Valley found its productive soil, the lush grasses, the dense timber that provided sustenance and shelter for themselves and their beasts— and they stayed despite the incursions of Indians and the hardships incident to settling in a new country.

The river is red because it flows through a red clay that colors the water. In the stretch included in this Valley it is fed by many streams from the Texas side, the Choctaw and Bois d'arc Bayous, Sanders Creek and Upper and Lower Pine Creeks. On the Oklahoma side are the larger Washita, Blue, Boggy and Kiamichi Rivers. The flow from the upper river is largely controlled now by the Denison Dam and Lake Texoma, and made to generate power that turns countless wheels in industry and provides light for an area that once depended on pine knots and tallow dips.

Into this Valley came people from many states, some thought they were in Texas but found they were in an area claimed by Missouri Territory and then by Arkansas Territory when that part of Missouri was set up as a separate government. Some went further West or South, some stayed in the Valley, and when the boundary was definitely determined all were citizens of Texas.

THE RED RIVER

"Men travel far to see a city, but few seem curious about a river. Every river has, nevertheless, its individuality, its great silent interest. Every river has, moreover, its influence over the people who pass their lives within sight of its waters." —H. S. Merriman

THOUGH the Valley was on the whole a desirable region in which to live, it had some of the disadvantages that hampered other sections of the country — floods and drouths, weather extremes—and for more than half a century an impediment to navigation by boats of considerable size, though oddly enough it made traffic with smaller boats possible.

It was the Red River Raft, an accumulation of trees washed into the river by floods that caved the banks or cut new channels, and lodged in the river about Shreveport. How long the Raft had been in the river no one could tell. The earliest comers were told by Indians that their fathers had told them it was there when they came in the early years of the Nineteenth Century. In some parts of the obstruction large trees grew, and while the lower end of the Raft was whittled away the upper end was being added to until at the time the Valley began to be peopled the Raft was estimated to be a hundred miles long "by the river", meaning the bends and loops the Red River makes in its course.

Between 1828 and 1841 the Federal government spent nearly half a million dollars on trying to destroy the Raft. Army engineers hacked at it on the lower end while the upper end was receiving more trees and other debris brought down by floods. It seemed a hopeless task.

While the Raft blocked the main channel of the river the water found its way around the obstruction, making "chutes" and bayous through which small steamboats could and did pass, and which were kept clear of obstructions by the boat owners and operators. This allowed the boats to come up to Jonesboro and the mouth of the Kiamichi River and in time of high water they went as far up as some landings in Fannin County.

[3]

These boats, in the time they were in the river, from the 'thirties to the later 'seventies of the last century, carried cotton, wheat, hides and other products of the Valley to Shreveport and New Orleans, and brought up merchandise of every sort. Travis Wright, whose early navigation had been by keel boats, had steamboats that operated from Wright's landing, opposite the mouth of the Kiamichi River where he had a store. Sam Fulton, who had a trading post on Red River north of where now is Paris, owned and operated boats and was interested in lines of boats on the Mississippi River. They made fairly regular trips except when there was an unusual lack of rainfall to put water in the river.

The river had made a chain of lakes above Shreveport that allowed boats to get to Jefferson, Texas, and in the years following the war between the sections Jefferson was the source of supply for most of the south side of the Valley, products being hauled there by ox teams and merchandise brought by the steamboats hauled back to the towns in the Valley. In 1873 the Raft was so nearly cleared that boats went through a continuous channel, and by 1880 the river was cleared except that snag pulling had to be continued.

The coming of the railroads put an end to navigation of the river through the Valley. Even before that, the cutting of the Raft in 1873 had so lowered the water in the bayous and lakes which made Jefferson a port that it was only in seasons of very high water that town could be reached, and presently it began to be reduced in population and business. Some steamboat men said the Raft was cut by demand of the railroads, but that of course was just talk.

As late as 1900 there was concerted action by citizens of the Valley to have the river improved by snag pulling and some sand bar removal, so that boats could be used to combat what was considered too high rates on the railroads. There was a small appropriation and some work was done

[4]

but presently it was abandoned when Army engineers reported the project was not economically sound.

Red River has had many floods, the greatest on record being in May, 1908, when the government gauge at Arthur City measured 43 feet, 5 inches above low water and the bridge of the Frisco Rail Road barely escaped destruction. The highest before that flood was in 1843, when it was said to have reached 38 feet. There were no gauges on the river then, but the old-timers apparently had a way of measuring the flood. That flood was in January. Travis Wright who lived on Jonesboro Prairie said the river was higher than he had ever seen it, and he had lived near it more than twenty-five years. He lost some baled cotton and some livestock, and part of the Jabez Fitzgerald distillery in Fannin County was washed away.

The flood of 1908 cut a new channel west of Arthur City, going far into Oklahoma, and leaving the old channel in front of what had been Sam Fulton's trading post a dry gulch, where great trees grow today. It washed away several valuable farms lower down the river, destroyed some small houses and drowned much livestock.

The first bridge that spanned the river in the Valley was that of the Katy Rail Road into Denison, followed by one lower down at Fulton, Arkansas, later by the Frisco Rail Road bridge at Arthur City and still later by other rail roads and many highway bridges.

There have been extremes of temperature more than once since records have been kept in the Valley. Several times there has been continued cold that covered the river with ice so thick that wagons were driven across. There have been hot seasons when no rain fell and vegetation withered, but there has never been what is considered a crop failure. Short crops, yes, but not a complete lack of production such as some sections have had and that some still have at intervals.

The winter of 1859-60 was unusually cold, Spring came

[5]

slowly. There was a good rain May 12, and not another drop fell over a large area of the Valley until August 15, 1860. Corn fell in the fields and the little produced brought $2.50 the bushel. North and South Sulphur Rivers south of the Valley were dry and cattle, cows and calves were driven to Red River for water by people in the counties bordering the river. Flour sold for $4.50 to $5 per 100 pounds, and a miller in Grayson County was paying $2 for wheat and selling flour to the Government for $7 per 100. Bacon was selling at 25 cents and was scarce.

The coldest weather recorded was Sunday, February 12, 1899, when the mercury in official thermometers fell to 15 below zero. The drop in temperature began in the afternoon of the day before, reached zero early in the night and did not get above zero until midday Monday.

Despite these extremes of temperature, the floods and the drouths, the Valley never had to cry for help because of them. The people accepted life as it came and knew that when things were at the worst they would get better. It is that spirit that has animated the people of the Valley from the beginning and during the first hundred years of its settlement.

SOME PIONEERS

"Shall I tell you who he is, this key figure in the arch of our enterprise? That slender, dauntless, plodding, modest figure is the American pioneer . . . His is this one glory—he found the way."
—Franklin K. Lane

Pecan Point and Jonesboro

Davy Crockett and Others

MEN WHO CAME to the Valley in the earliest years of the period included in these stories stopped mostly on the north side of Red River, where Arkansas was exercising jurisdiction, with courts functioning after a fashion. Apparently they did not think they were in Texas, which then was Spanish territory. They made settlements at Pecan Point and Clear Creek and on the prairies bordering the river. Some stayed briefly and went on into Texas, while others remained longer, crossing Red River when they were ordered to move to make the land clear for the Indians who were to come from east of the Mississippi River.

They were all sorts of people—good, bad and worse. Thomas Nuttall, the naturalist, made a trip through the country with Major William Bradford from Fort Smith in 1819, when he was sent to move the squatters from the public lands. Of the Clear Creek settlement Nuttall said, "These people . . . bear the worst moral character imaginable, many of them being renegades from justice. . . When a further flight from justice became necessary they passed over into Spanish territory, toward San Antonio, where it appears encouragement was given all sorts of refugees." William Dewees, who lived about Clear Creek two years before going to South Texas, agreed with Nuttall. Both however, recorded the backwoodsmen were hospitable and courageous and were wringing subsistence from the wilderness.

There were some good people among them—men who had not come a little ahead of an officer with a warrant, but who had brought their families, looking for a home—such men as Claiborne Wright, Henry Stout, William Ragsdale, Nathaniel Robbins, Joseph Inglish, Daniel Davis and many others, who became leaders of men to fight Indians in Texas when the savages made incursions in the Valley, and the sons of whom became important figures in Texas in later years. [9]

Most of these people came overland, those from Missouri and Arkansas riding horses or mules or driving oxen. Some from states east of the Mississippi River came to Little Rock on boats and thence overland. Some trappers and traders came in canoes on Red River.

The Federal government had agreed with Indians in Mississippi and adjacent states to trade their lands for lands in what was to be Indian Territory. In 1819 Major William Bradford came from Fort Smith under orders from Andrew Jackson, commander of Southern Division of United States Army, and moved all squatters who were on the north of Red River and west of the Kiamichi River. Those east of the Kiamichi were to be given extension of time to gather crops already growing.

But in 1820 Captain Combs came from Natchitoches and moved the settlers who were east of the Kiamichi, destroying crops that were not ready for harvest, and burning their houses. This was something the people had not expected and so indignant were they that Captain Combs had to take to his boat, which had a guard of soldiers, and go back down the river. The men and boys followed along the river bank, trying to get a chance to kill Combs, but he did not show himself. While he was being followed, some Indians came into the settlements and stole everything they could carry off.

When the people on the north side of Red River had been forced out, and it was certain the area was a part of Indian Territory, the Miller County, Arkansas, court house, that had been at Shawneetown, a few miles nearer the river than present-day Idabel, Oklahoma, was abandoned. The county seat was moved to Jonesboro, a village on the south side of Red River, several miles west of Pecan Point's principal settlement.

Jonesboro was a sizeable village, laid out with wide streets, several stores and residences. Claiborne Wright had been elected sheriff of Miller County and lived in Jonesboro.   [10]

Through the village came many of the people who were to settle in the Valley or go further into Texas. To Jonesboro came Stephen Austin, and talked with Wright about routes into Texas for his colonists. He was advised to bring them through Nacogdoches as they would be nearer to the lands they were to occupy, there would be fewer streams to cross, and the trails were better. Sam Houston came through Jonesboro on his way to southern Texas and was entertained by James Clark. David Crockett, on the way from Tennessee to San Antonio, crossed the river at Jonesboro.

Crockett traveled south to about where now is Clarksville, visited some people he had known in Tennessee who had preceded him to Texas and settled. Then he angled southwest to the home of Matthias Click, who had left Miller County some years before and was living on his land several miles south of where now is Paris. At Click's he spent some time, going west over the prairies as far as what is now Grayson County. He was hunting buffalo and near where now is Honey Grove, in Fannin County, he found wild bees and honey so abundant that he wrote his children about it, and the city of Honey Grove takes its name from Crockett's discovery.

Matt Click had come from Tennessee and stopped for a time in the Pecan Point settlements. He had come into Texas in 1834 and he and his sons took their headrights in what is now southern Lamar County. There Click built a two-story log house, with one-story wings, not far from Aud's Creek, and entertained travelers who were becoming numerous. When Crockett had satisfied his hunting desire and left Click's he went to San Augustine, then to San Antonio—and death. One of Matt Click's sons, even after he had grown to be an old man, was so prone to tell of Davy Crockett's visit with his father, that people began to call him "Davy Crockett" Click, and he liked it.

The Skidmore family, who settled not far from the

[*11*]

Clicks later, were friends of Crockett in Tennessee. One of the sons, Henry Skidmore, who spent his life in Lamar County and was a respected citizen, said he and Crockett had agreed to come to Texas together. They were to meet at a designated place and time, but by some mischance Skidmore was delayed, or Crockett was ahead of time. When Skidmore reached the place, Crockett had gone. Skidmore followed but never caught up with Davy, though he found the ashes of what had been Crockett's camp fires in several places on the trail. When Skidmore reached Lamar County, which then was a part of Red River County, Crockett had gone and Skidmore followed him no farther.

There were many other pioneers, some of whom are told of in other parts of this story of the Valley. Some came direct to Texas after it had gained independence, but while the Valley was still largely unexplored, and finding it to their liking they settled and spent their lives.

PECAN POINT, the Anglicized name for the Punta Pecana of the Spaniards who first traveled the Valley, was not a settlement in the usually accepted meaning of the term. It was rather a sort of stopping place, a large area on both sides of the Red River. It was there that Claiborne Wright and his family stopped in the Fall of 1816, after six months spent on a keel boat, coming from Carthage, Tennessee. Some trappers and traders had preceded Wright, and two other families arrived about the same time.

Some of these people thought they were in Texas, which then was a part of Mexico. They found they were in Arkansas, so far as paying taxes and being haled to court. For eight years Arkansas claimed the area north of the river, and continued its claim and its exercise of jurisdiction over the area on the south side for more than twenty years, relinquishing it only when the boundary between

[12]

the Republic of Texas and United States was surveyed and determined.

Just two years after Wright arrived, William M. Jones started a settlement on the south bank of the river a little below the mouth of the Kiamichi River, which presently became a town with streets and lots where were homes and stores.

Jones' wife was a sister of Judge Gabriel N. Martin, whom Jones persuaded later to join him on Red River.

Across the river there were scattered small settlements of people who had squatted and who were removed when the treaty with the Choctaw and other Indian tribes of the South was made and preparations began for the coming of the Indians to their new lands.

Some of the settlers were tough by preference and practice; others by force of circumstances in order to hold their own with the outlaws and drifters. Gradually the better element prevailed, and though there was lawlessness in the Valley it was no greater than in any other frontier region.

The area claimed by Arkansas on both sides of the river was styled Miller County, and courts were held in the house of Claiborne Wright, on the north side of the river, a few miles south of where now is Idabel, county seat of McCurtain County, Oklahoma. This served for eight or nine years. When Arkansas was finally convinced that the area north of the river was not a part of its territory, the court was moved to Jonesboro on the south bank of the river, where it continued until Texas gained freedom from Mexico.

Not all the immigrants who came during the first twenty years stayed at Pecan Point or Jonesboro. Some went down to South Texas where Austin was settling colonists. Others went further west into what Texas called Red River County—an indefinitely described area that reached far beyond present-day Grayson County. Mostly

[13]

they were men with families, seeking homes, and found desirable sites which presently became villages, then towns and cities. The north side of the Valley was the home of the Indians, into which white people gradually filtered, until it, too, was made into a Territory, then a State, and given a place in the Union.

Some of the men answered the call from Washington-on-the-Brazos and represented Red River district in signing the Declaration of Independence and the Constitution. They were Richard Ellis, Robert Hamilton, Collin McKinney, Albert Latimer and Samuel Carson. Others went to help fight the Mexicans but reached South Texas too late to get in the battle of San Jacinto. One of them was George W. Wright, son of Claiborne Wright, who worked as a courier for General Sam Houston for a time, and was elected a Representative to the First Texas Congress for Red River County.

A considerable number of settlers arriving in 1836 had gone west of the Bois d'arc Bayou, and for them the travel to court which was held at LaGrange, a village northeast of present day Clarksville, was too great a journey. This was remedied by the second Congress dividing Red River County, and making all west of Bois d'arc Bayou into a county named Fannin, with court to be held at Warren, a settlement which had been a trading post on Red River. The Fifth Congress continued dividing Red River County, making two additional counties, that nearest the Arkansas line being called Bowie, and the western third, adjoining Fannin County, being called Lamar. The Congress named chief justices for each county who called elections for other officials—sheriff, county and district clerks, surveyor and coroner. County seats were selected by the voters, court houses were built, and the southern part of the Valley had become, in fact as well as in name, a part of the Republic of Texas.

All the counties changed their county seats one or more

[*14*]

times. Red River County selected Clarksville instead of LaGrange; Fannin moved from Warren to Bois d'arc, afterwards called Bonham; Lamar selected a place northwest of Paris and called it Lafayette, then moved to another called Mount Vernon, south of Paris, finally selecting Paris; Bowie chose Boston instead of DeKalb, and Grayson moved its first Sherman a few miles east to where it now is.

The Oklahoma constitutional convention in 1907 created the counties and named the county seats in that state, those in the Valley being McCurtain, with Idabel as county seat; Choctaw, with Hugo as county seat; and Durant was made county seat of Bryan County.

INDIANS AND SETTLERS

And laying in every bog and bush
As still as a snake in hiding,
Hunting the covey they had to flush,
The Indians come like a rattler's rush
A-slithering and a-sliding.
—*Martha Keller,"Brady's Bend"*
[*By permission Rutgers University Press*]

Some Encounters that Stained
the Soil of the Valley

THE PORTION of the Valley included in the area of these stories had few Indians living in it during the years the settlers were coming. It had been the home of the Caddo tribe from time immemorial until about 1795 when the Osages came down from the north and almost exterminated the less-warlike Caddos. During the years following the early settlement of 1816, the Osages made raids at intervals, and in the western part of the area the worst depredations were made by bands of Indians who had emigrated from the United States in 1822 and 1824 and lived in the country bordering the Trinity River and between that stream and Red River. They were called the Cherokees and their twelve associated bands, being composed of members of that number of tribes.

At first there was little trouble by these Indians but as some of them began stealing horses and plundering houses in the absence of the family, the settlers retaliated until there was open and often bloody warfare. It was worse in the west part of the Valley which had been created into Fannin County, and in the eastern section where the first settlers had located. There are only two known instances of tragedies in what is now Lamar County. Several families had stopped near the mouth of Upper Pine Creek and in the absence of some of the men the Osages raided the settlement and killed most of the people. The absent men returning from a hunt pursued the Indians and were themselves killed.

In 1840 Indians attacked the home of the Featherstone family in what is now southeast Lamar County, while the husband was absent, killed Mrs. Featherstone and a Negro woman, leaving their bodies in the yard and burning the house. Some men in the neighborhood followed their trail for a while but the Indians had too long a start and were never punished.

[*19*]

Several forts had been built by settlers. They were log buildings, used also as homes, and built so as to afford protection from Indians. One was at Bois d'arc (now Bonham) in Fannin County, built by Bailey Inglish. Another was not far from where is now the town of Ben Franklin, Delta County, built by a group on the Jacob Lyday headright, and another was built by Jesse Shelton in what is now southwestern Lamar County. They served as refuges for women and children while the men were hunting on the trail of Indian raiders or working in their fields.

A few notable affairs will serve to show partly what these early settlers had to go through. Judge Gabriel Martin married Henrietta, a daughter of Claiborne Wright, in 1825, at Jonesboro. Judge Martin had a large plantation in Red River County and was fond of hunting. In the Spring of 1834, with his son Matthew, then about eight years old, and two Negro slaves, one a boy about Matt's age and the other grown, he went several miles west of Fort Towson on the north side of the river. Their camp was attacked by Pawnee Indians from the west, Judge Martin was killed, the older Negro hid in a hollow log, and Matt and the Negro boy were taken by the Indians. Because the little Negro cried and made a fuss the Indians killed him.

Travis Wright, uncle of the boy, and oldest living son of Claiborne Wright, who had died in 1830, traded for some Pawnee Indians who had been captured by another tribe in a fight, and with them set out for the Pawnee village. General Henry Leavenworth was then in command at Fort Gibson and there Travis Wright asked assistance. The General detailed Colonel G. M. Dodge with 200 men to go with Wright and at the Pawnee village, on the headwaters of one branch of Red River, Wright traded his prisoners for the boy Matt and a Negro man who had been captured in another raid and had been

[20]

kind to the boy. George Wright was made guardian for Matt, who was educated in Clarksville schools and lived a part of his life in Lamar County, dying unmarried in 1868.

LATE IN 1840 the house of John Yeary in what is now southern Fannin County was attacked by ten Indians while Yeary and his Negro man were at work in the field. Mrs. Yeary stood in the door with a gun in her hands and Yeary and the Negro, armed only with hoes, ran toward her. They got over the yard fence and went at the Indians. Yeary was struck by an arrow over one eye, the point glancing around the skull, and Mrs. Yeary was wounded in the hip while coming to bring Yeary the gun. When they saw he had the gun the Indians ran.

Yeary felled several of the Indians with his hoe before the handle broke and he then fought with his fists. An Indian sitting behind a stump was snapping an old flint-lock gun and Yeary called to him that he would be attended to as soon as he got through with the others, and the Indian seemed to understand for he also ran. Yeary called after them that he could whip a hundred of them, then turned to the Negro and said, "Tony, we will knock off for the day."

When they went in the house and found Mrs. Yeary wounded the old man was so mad he said he would have killed all of them if he had known she was hurt. He sent Tony to Colonel William Bourland's a few miles away to get help to attend to Mrs. Yeary and Bourland was angry because they had not called him to fight the Indians. Tony said he did not think Colonel Bourland had a right to be mad for he and old Master had no time to do anything except fight until they were all gone.

IN THE LATE 'FORTIES Joseph Houndshell lived in what is southeastern Lamar County. One day when he was ab-

[21]

sent and Mrs. Houndshell was busy in the house, a Negro woman doing the family wash in the yard squalled and "Aunt Mary" went to the door. An Indian was climbing over the fence after he had shot the Negro woman with an arrow that was sticking in that part of her body most exposed when she leaned over the tub. He evidently thought she was the only person on the place and that he could come in and take what he wanted. "Aunt Mary" was a different proposition and when the Indian saw her in the door he started to run. She stepped back, grabbed Old Betsy off the hooks on the wall, stepped out and fired at him but failed to hit him, and he galloped off, clearing the tops of the bushes in his leaps to get away.

IN APRIL, 1841, Indians murdered the Ripley family in Titus County, and it was determined the murderers had come from the west, probably on the Trinity. Citizens gathered at Choctaw Bayou and formed a company to hunt these Indians. They chose James Bourland as captain, but General E. H. Tarrant, officer in the militia and experienced Indian fighter, was among the company and was accepted as the actual leader. The party numbered fewer than a hundred. Going to the west fork of the Trinity they passed through the lower Cross Timbers and crossed the middle fork of the Trinity. Next day they came to a deserted village of sixty-odd empty lodges which they destroyed with axes, fearing that the smoke if they were burned would bring Indians on them in an unfavorable place.

Changing direction they were two days later on the Trinity near where now is Fort Worth and scouts found villages a few miles in front. They swept through one village and found there were two others. The men were becoming scattered and Tarrant gave John B. Denton, a scout leader, permission to go after the Indians who had gone toward the river. With Henry Stout, another scout leader, and their groups, they followed the Indians. Denton was shot and killed and Stout was wounded. Seeing from the number of lodges in the villages that there were at least a thousand Indians, the body of Denton was put on a horse and the men started on the return to Fannin County. Denton was buried after they had gone a few miles from what was called the Village Creek fight. In 1860 John Chisum, ranching in Denton County, employed Henry Stout to find Denton's burial place, and Chisum moved the bones and reburied them in his ranch yard. Forty-one years later, citizens of Denton had the bones again dug up, and reburied them in the City of Denton.

IN FANNIN COUNTY John Kitchens lived near Red River. He refused to go into better settled country and determined to make corn. Indians had marked him and made several attempts to kill him, but failed. They burned some of the fence around his corn field and one day they saw the old man and his son start to the woods to make rails to replace the fence to keep deer out of the corn. Kitchens and his son carried nothing but their tools. The Indians divided, some went after Kitchens, others attacked the house where were the mother and two girls. The old man and his son killed three Indians with the axes and wedges and the others dispersed. Hearing the noise at the house, where the women were shooting, they found five Indians and a Negro man down, and the others in flight. The chronicler of this story, Judge J. P. Simpson, said Indians never attacked that place again, as they feared the axes and wedges.

LATER CAME SOME Osage Indians and attacked the early settlements on Sanders Prairie, and after robbing some houses were leaving when they came on the house of the Jansing family. Mrs. Jansing was alone, her husband having taken his gun and gone to visit a friend, but as no

[23]

sign of Indians had been seen, the woman was not afraid to be alone. More than a dozen of the Indians attacked the house where she had shut and barred the door. An Indian forced it open far enough to reach in for the bar and Mrs. Jansing promptly cut off the hand with her axe and she fastened the door more securely. Then she saw several Indians coming up through the loose puncheons that made the floor. She applied the axe to them and they retreated.

As told by Judge J. P. Simpson, Fannin County pioneer and official, Daniel Dugan lived some distance from Warren, a settlement on Red River. His son, Daniel, was killed by Indians while at work near the house. Then one night his house was attacked and one man, a visitor, was killed but the old man and his two sons fought them off. Next morning one Indian left dead in the yard was found to have on a calico shirt Dr. Daniel Rowlett, another pioneer, had given him some time before. Dugan's young daughter, Catherine, had vowed when her brother was killed, that she would cut off the head of the first Indian she got at. She made good on this one, chopping off his head with an axe. The skull, with the flesh taken off it, was kept about the house for years and Judge Simpson saw it there. It was hung at the side of the loom, and the old lady used it as a receptacle for the quills that were used in weaving.

There were countless other Indian depredations all through the Red River Valley during the years in which the country was being settled. These show the cruelty of the Indians and the hardihood of the men and women and even children who had come to the Valley to make their homes and who were determined to stay regardless of what might befall them.

Some Indians who had left their homes east of the Mississippi River to go to Indian Territory, later than the main body of those removed by the government, wandered into Texas, south of Red River, and stayed for a time. They were friendly and the settlers were glad to have them, believing they served to keep the warlike Indians from the west and north from raiding the settlements.

One small band settled on a creek near Pattonville in what is now southeast Lamar County. Others stopped in Red River County and their names were given to Delaware Creek that runs through Clarksville, Kickapoo Creek further east and Shawnee Prairie, in southeast Red River County. One Delaware was Chief Cuthand, who said he had lost his hand in the battle of Tippecanoe and there is a small creek named Cuthand Creek. A Shawnee chief was named Cowleach. These Indians were presently moved into the Indian Territory, as they had been killing some of the settlers' hogs that ran at large on the open range, the Indians thinking that anything found in the woods had no owner and could be killed for food.

FORT TOWSON AND DOAKSVILLE

The Goodings and Haddens

Indians at Home and Away

*Recollections of a Boy Who
Knew Them in Both Places*

FORT TOWSON, an Army post in Choctaw Nation, and its adjacent village, Doaksville, were important in affairs of the north side of the Valley for more than a quarter century. The first Fort Towson was a log structure and stockade near the mouth of the Kiamichi River. It was built in 1824 to protect the Indians who were expected to move into the Territory, from encroachment of the white settlers, and to aid the Choctaw and Chickasaw Indians, and the remnants of the Caddo and Delaware Tribes, from incursions of the Comanches and Kiowas from the west.

Immigration of the Indians from east of the Mississippi River had not begun, but there were many white people along the Kiamichi, on lands that had been set aside for the Indians, and the soldiers at the Fort had their hands full trying to keep them in order. There were many good people in that area, but there were also some tough characters as ever drew a pistol or wielded a knife.

The Indians still had not come by 1829, so the Fort was abandoned and presently was burned, probably by some of the disgruntled men who had been held to comparative decency while the soldiers were quartered there.

In 1831, Fort Towson was re-established, this time near Gates Creek, a small tributary of the Kiamichi. There it was built for permanence, with stone foundations for the squared log buildings which were covered with clapboards. Here for near twenty-five years a considerable force of soldiers was kept. The Choctaw and Chickasaw Indians began arriving and the soldiers at the Fort were needed.

Representatives of United States had met the Choctaw representatives in 1820 at Doak's Stand, on the old Natchez Trace, in Mississippi. When it was seen that the transfer of the Indians would really begin, the Doaks went to Indian Territory and set up a trading house, which became the village of Doaksville. Fort Towson was built about a mile and a half from the village, which began to grow. By 1850 it had several stores, a number of residences and, for a time, a small newspaper. Fort Towson was on the road from Fort Smith to Texas and was a pay station for distributing the Indians' annuities, as well as for the soldiers. The country having become pretty well settled by 1854, the Fort was again abandoned. It was left untended, and presently when it was used by the agent for the Choctaw and Chickasaw Indians it was found in need of repair, with few of the buildings habitable. Not long after this the buildings, except the hospital and a few small structures, burned.

During the early 'fifties Doaksville flourished. The little newspaper, in 1851, had advertisements of P. Colbert and of Berthelet & Jones, general merchandise. The Jones in the latter was Colonel Robert Jones, an Indian, who was wealthy and engaged in many enterprises. J. R. Bryant & Co. manufactured saddles and harness; Irving & Riddle were making wagons; Henry Hadden was doing sheet metal work and sold cook stoves; F. J. Murphy made daguerreotypes, "in the best manner."

The Army had surplus stores, even then. In October, 1851, Lieutenant M. R. Stevenson of Seventh Infantry, and AACS at the Fort, advertised to sell at auction 46 barrels of flour, 2 barrels pork, 430 pounds salt beef, 180 pounds ham, 10 barrels and 5 gallons of pickles. At the same time he was asking bids for furnishing 4,500 bushels of corn for horses at the Fort, which he bought for $87\frac{1}{2}$ to 95 cents a bushel.

The missionaries had schools and churches near the Fort and were welcomed there, where the morals of the men were said to be excellent, many of them being church members. The family of George Gooding, who was sutler at the Fort, lived in a house outside the enclosure of the

[30]

Fort and was much respected. Mr. Gooding was born in Maine and had been a sutler with the Army many years. He died in his home in 1851, and was buried with Masonic ceremony by Doaksville Lodge, of which he was a charter member. He had been sutler at the Fort since its establishment.

One of George Gooding's sons, Lawrence, was about seventeen years old when Captain R. B. Marcy went on his first expedition to Santa Fe to map a route for people going to the California gold fields, and he allowed Lawrence to accompany the party. After his father's death Lawrence Gooding, known to his friends as "Larry," went to Paris, Texas, worked in newspaper offices as a printer, and was himself a publisher a short time. During the war between the sections he printed the small "change bills" for Lamar County, the Confederate government issuing nothing smaller than $5 bills. When advanced in years Larry went to Durant, Oklahoma, where one of his sons was in business, and Larry died there some years later. His sister, Carrie Gooding, married Basil LeFlore, a Choctaw who became principal chief of the Choctaw Nation. They lived for a time, after the Fort was abandoned, at Goodland, where Mrs. LeFlore taught in the mission school which was near their home.

The LeFlore house, one room of hewed logs and a lean-to, was built in 1838. Almost a hundred years later the land on which it stood was bought and added to the Goodland school and orphanage. The house was taken apart, the material carried to the school campus, and it was rebuilt, exactly as it was first built, to be used as a museum. It also was a memorial to Mrs. Annie Schooler, deceased wife of W. E. Schooler, Hugo, Oklahoma, newspaper publisher, who with his wife had long been interested in the welfare of the school and orphanage, the removal and reconstruction cost being paid by Mr. Schooler.

The Henry Hadden home in Doaksville was the social

[*31*]

center of the village for some years, before the family moved to Paris, Texas, after the Fort burned in the late 'fifties. Henry Hadden was born in Pennsylvania. His sister married Captain McDermott, an officer in the United States Army. McDermott was sent West and his wife and her brother went with him to Fort Gibson, then to Fort Smith and to Fort Towson. Hadden followed his trade of sheet metal worker. After going to Doaksville he met an Irish girl, Mary Tobin, at Fort Towson, and he courted and married her.

Mary Tobin came from Ireland to New York when a child to be with her sister who had married a soldier stationed in Brooklyn. Mary took employment as a domestic when her sister's husband was sent to the West and assigned to Fort Towson. The sister wanted Mary with her and the girl made the journey by steamers from Pittsburgh to Fort Smith, then by stage to Fort Towson, only to find that her brother-in-law had been sent to Algiers, Louisiana, and his wife had gone with him. Mary was taken care of by Captain Willard, commandant at the Fort, and there Henry Hadden met and married her.

Hadden was a man of excellent character, an elder in the Presbyterian Church, and his family was reared and educated properly. His move to Paris was made in order to take advantage of the good schools, as Doaksville was declining in the late 'fifties, after the Fort burned. In Paris he followed his trade, bought a home and for years was a prominent citizen.

Hadden's oldest son, named Henry, was a playmate of the Gooding children at Fort Towson, and was a favorite with the officers and men at the Fort, as well as with the Indians who came to Doaksville. When grown he became a railroad locomotive engineer and after retiring spent his last years in Springfield, Missouri, where he passed away when nearly ninety years old.

After retiring he wrote for me some reminiscences of

[32]

his early life with the Indians and told, in his simple words, a striking story of life in and around Doaksville and Fort Towson. Henry said that when the Indians came to Doaksville or Fort Towson they rode horses that were really ponies; that an Indian never walked if he could get something to ride. It was amusing, he said, to see a big Indian on one of the small ponies, moving very slowly, always with a rifle across the saddle in front and his feet almost dragging the ground. If he was married, his wife walked behind him, carrying the latest baby.

Indian women came to Doaksville peddling. They made baskets of many sizes and patterns, which they carried in a large basket slung to their shoulders with a hickory withe. Some brought needlework, such as beaded moccasins, and bed quilts; others offered berries or fruits or home-baked food, such as barbecued corn, hominy and bunny-ha. Mrs. Hadden traded them salt or sugar for such things as she wanted which they had for sale or barter. The men, white and red, had much time for play, and pitched horseshoes or played marbles.

The Hadden family moved to Paris when Henry was ten years old. Several times he went back to the Nation with his father on business or visiting old friends. On one of these visits they spent the night with the Reverend O. P. Stark, mission teacher at Goodland. War had been declared between the North and South, and the Choctaws had decided to fight with the South. A big war council was held. The Indians were full of gin. One sat on the ground at the foot of a flag pole, beating a big bass drum. Then another drum was heard in the distance, some of the Indians got on their ponies and rode in that direction. When the two groups met there was a great pow wow that sounded to Henry like turkeys gobbling.

Several other drums were heard, and as each group arrived at the council ground they began to take part in the council. After dark there was a war dance by the

[*33*]

younger men, consisting of a lot of red paint and feathers and much yelling. The idea seemed to Henry to be to show their ability to kick, jump, twist and turn, as they moved sideways around the flag pole, and the man who kept beating the big drum. After the bucks were exhausted the squaws came and stood in a circle, each pair facing and each carrying a gun and chanting as they took mincing steps.

Henry said his father reared his family as a member of the Presbyterian Church should. When he was about seven years old, at Doaksville, there was to be an execution under Indian law, Doaksville being the site of one of their courts. The jail and execution place was less than a hundred yards from the Hadden home and the father did not want the boy to see the execution. Early that morning his father told Henry they would go for a ride in the country. The father got on his horse, took the boy up behind him, and they rode out of town, meeting on the road many men coming in to see the execution. After a long ride the father and son returned, came in home the back way, put the horse in the stable and went into the house. Henry saw his mother standing at a window, looking through the blind slats, and boy-like he went up and peeped out just in time to see the sheriff take aim and shoot the condemned man. So, he said, "I got the ride and to see the execution too."

Henry said about all the prayer he knew at that time was "Now I lay me," so when there came a big wind one day, filling the air with dust and bending the trees, he ran into the house and feeling the need for prayer began crying, "Holy Moses, Holy Moses," recollecting his Sunday School lessons about Moses and his narrow escapes. Soon the wind stopped and after a while they learned the tornado had destroyed the buildings at Pine Ridge Mission, a few miles from Doaksville. Feathers were blown off chickens and other pranks of tornadoes had been demonstrated, but none of the mission people was injured.

The Indians liked to play jokes, too, especially the young men. One Sunday, when Henry was about five years old, his father put him on a pony, and he and his father, the latter on a horse, rode down to the garrison creek to water the horse and pony. Coming back they had got near home and Henry found himself lying on the ground and a big Indian in war paint and feathers picking him up. There was a bunch of them decked out that way. They put him back on his pony and had a big laugh. They had been down to the Red River where doggeries were on the Texas side and drank enough to make them foolish. Those dumps along the Texas and Arkansas borders were a curse to the Indians, Henry said, and caused many brawls, stabbings and sometimes murders.

The Folsom family, Henry said, were prominent Indians and well-to-do. They favored Bible names, the brothers being Israel, Samson, Daniel, Simeon, Noah and Isaac. He went with his father to see Noah Folsom who was at Sim's house. They uncovered Noah and Henry saw shocking knife wounds, great stabs and slashes. Noah was about twenty-five and big and handsome. He soon died. The men there said the trouble came from drinking and gambling. Noah had a fine horse, flax mane and tail, which Henry had seen. He was told that the horse was killed and buried with Noah and his gun and some food for use in the happy hunting grounds.

Noah Folsom was killed by W. E. Gildast, a white man, in April, 1855. A document in the archives in Washington contains testimony that Indian Agent D. H. Cooper took on examination. It indicated the two men were playing cards and drinking in a store, a quarrel arose between them and Gildast killed Folsom with a butcher knife.

Samson Folsom had a fine plantation on Horse Prairie and Henry said he used to visit there with his parents, and it was wonderful. In the yard was a great iron pot on a

[35]

stone foundation and fire could be made under it. Sometimes the overseer, a white man, would have the Negro slaves get out the big seine, that was perhaps a hundred feet long. With half a dozen Negro men and the seine in a wagon they would drive down to Red River, fasten one end of the seine to a stump, stretch out the other end, everybody strip and wade in with the end of the seine, make a half circle, hitch a mule to the end of the seine and haul it in, with more fish than the boy had ever seen.

Up at the house lard was put in the big kettle, some cleaned fish, some baked cornbread, some made coffee, and the white folks, Indians and Negroes feasted on fish and corn dodgers until it was time for bed.

After the Haddens moved to Paris they were often visited by Indians they had known while living at Doaksville. The Sam Folsom family came often, Henry said. They rode in a carriage, with servants following in a wagon which was used to take back the supplies they bought in Paris. The servants were to wait on the Folsoms while visiting so as to not burden their hosts. Other Indians would come singly or in pairs. Henry thought it comical to see an Indian riding slowly, his rifle across the saddle in front and a deer tied across the back of the saddle, coming down the main street and turning in at the Hadden home. The Indians wanted the venison cooked their way, which was to cut a steak, lay it in a hot skillet with little if any grease and cook very dry. Mrs. Hadden made hominy for their visitors, cooked it in the ashes until the hulls came off the corn and set it in a jar by the fireplace. Sometimes it would sour, but the Indians seemed to like it that way. They called it ton-sha-pa-sho-pa.

Many Choctaw Indians did their buying in Paris after Fort Towson was abandoned and Doaksville faded. They sometimes came in wagons, a regular train, with some riding horseback. Several merchants in Paris then— Charles Thebo, Travis Wright, Isaiah Wells—had been merchants in or near Doaksville and the Indians knew them and traded with them. After the Indians arrived in Paris and put their teams in a wagon yard they would go the rounds of the stores, look at everything and buy supplies. They could get whisky in Paris, and in all other Texas towns then, the sale of which was unlawful in the Nation, and sometimes one would drink too much.

The women usually bought bright red and yellow calico, often a whole bolt, and the more prosperous bought ribbons and jewelry. The men were fond of jewelry, too, especially fine gold watches. They bought boots, saddles, fine spurs, blankets, and suits of clothes, and almost all bought groceries.

Henry said his father was kept busy helping Indians out of trouble in Paris. A full-blood who could speak no English might be set upon by hoodlums who had taken on too much liquor. Sometimes they would take his pony, claiming he had stolen it. The Indian would tell his friend, Mr. Hadden, of his trouble and Hadden would go to the rescue, perhaps have to get a lawyer and go through court procedure, to get back a pony worth perhaps five dollars.

COLONEL ROBERT M. JONES

*Choctaw Indian
Whose Career Ranged from Peddler to
Owner of Plantations, Slaves
and Steamboats*

ONE OF THE MOST SPECTACULAR figures in the Choctaw Nation during the years following the migration from Mississippi, was Colonel Robert M. Jones. His death was followed by litigation over property rights that was drawn out more than ten years, and indirectly brought on two tragedies.

Robert M. Jones was a Choctaw Indian, born in 1808, who came to Indian Territory about 1836, after many of his people had traveled the "Trail of Tears." Years after his death his daughter said her father began by peddling merchandise through the country, buying in New Orleans and trading for hides, furs and other produce. He made money recovering stolen children from wild Indian tribes by reason of the rewards paid by their relatives. As he made money he invested it so that by the time of the war between the sections he was wealthy. He owned five hundred Negro slaves, several steamboats on Red River, and five plantations along the river from near the Arkansas line to Lake West, in present Bryan County, Oklahoma.

Showing Colonel Jones' operations as a trader and financier, is the record in Lamar County, Texas, made in 1847, of a bill of sale Colonel Jones received from John McDonough of New Orleans, transferring to Jones two plantations in Indian Territory, all their equipment and livestock and produce, (except cotton in bales) and 56 Negroes. All the Negroes were named in the bill of sale, except "Nan's child," the whole transaction amounting to $20,000, on which Jones paid $5,000 and gave notes for the remainder. And this was the Choctaw Indian peddler who in fifteen years had accumulated a fortune that was the larger part of a million dollars, and while doing so retained the respect of the people who knew him.

Colonel Jones' first wife died in 1860 and was buried at Rose Hill, a plantation where he had built her a house

[*41*]

that was the finest residence in the Territory or North Texas. The place is about five miles southeast of present-day Hugo, Oklahoma. Of their five children only one survived the mother. She had married Robert Love and had two sons, Robert M. and Arthur Love.

In the 'fifties of the last century Colonel Jones owned a store in Doaksville in partnership with J. R. Berthelet, who was also post master there, the larger interest in a store in Paris, Texas, under the name of C. F. Thebo & Company, and various other enterprises. When the war came on he supported the Confederacy and was the delegate from Choctaw Nation to the Confederate Congress in Richmond. He was a charter member of the Doaksville Masonic Lodge, the first organized in Indian Territory, and he gave material support to the missionaries who were teaching and preaching to his people. Colonel Jones died in February, 1873, with much of his fortune gone, his slaves freed and many of his debtors made bankrupt by the war.

Some years after his wife's death, Colonel Jones married a woman from the North who was a teacher in one of the mission schools. For her he built in Paris, Texas, on a twelve-acre lot, a residence so magnificent for those days that it was known over North Texas as the Jones Mansion. It was built in the late 'sixties, of finest materials, the door and window frames and finishings being brought from New Orleans by steamer to Jefferson and hauled to Paris on wagons. Two children had been born to the second wife, a son, Robert Jr., and a daughter, Mary. The family lived in the mansion only part time and apparently did not like it, for about 1871 it was listed as the capital prize in a proposed "gift concert" or lottery, promoted by a group of North Texas men, the advertisement setting its value at $35,000. The concert or drawing was never held and one night in 1872 the mansion burned while the family was absent in Choctaw Nation.

The second Mrs. Jones filed application to probate her husband's will, it having been already filed in the Choctaw court. The will, made about a year before Colonel Jones' death, made provision for his first wife's daughter (who in the meantime, after Love's death, had married a man named Ruty), for the Love boys, and for the second wife and the two children. The Paris mansion lot had been bought for Mrs. Jones and the deed was in her name, so it was not a part of the estate. There was about $30,000 life insurance and large amounts claimed to be owed to Colonel Jones by several persons, most of which was never collected. The litigation as usual resulted in attorney's fees and court costs that ate at the assets until there was little left.

Some time after Colonel Jones died the widow married Dr. S. W. Bailey, the family physican, and one of the witnesses to Jones' will. Dr. Bailey was killed early in 1882, in an altercation over ownership of a list of cotton grown on one of the plantations, but the litigation went on. Mrs. Love-Ruty claimed the legacies left her and her sons had not been paid. Mrs. Jones' daughter, Mary, had married George Randell, a resident of Denison, Texas, and she also sued for her share of the estate. Her claim was settled by transferring to her the mansion lot in Paris in exchange for her interest in the Rose Hill home place.

After Ruty died his widow, who had been Mrs. Love, married Tom Paine. His death, like that of Dr. Bailey, was a tragedy. Tom Paine was a son of the Reverend F. M. Paine, a preacher and respected citizen of Paris in the years following the war between the sections. Tom seems to have been the proverbial black sheep of an otherwise good family. He became what was called a professional gambler, making his income, if any, by being a better poker player than his opponents. Tom was good looking and dressed, as did all such characters then, in the height of fashion. He went over to Choctaw Nation and there married Mrs. Ruty. She and her sons, the Love boys, had been willed a considerable part of the estate by her father and Tom Paine apparently saw himself as a landed gentleman, which was much better than poker playing.

Tom is said to have taken charge of the plantation, and in fact of the whole neighborhood, as his sort in those days were supremely self-confident and had an overweening idea of their own importance. One day he learned that some Indians employed on the plantation were cutting timber, supposedly by order of Mrs. Paine, who had been operating the plantation very well before marrying Tom. He objected to the timber cutting, went to the stable and finding no horse available mounted a mule. Armed with his trusty Colt's six-gun, a mark of votaries of chance as well as of some substantial citizens then, he rode to where the timber was being cut, and in language profane and vigorous, demanded the cutting stop.

His command was obeyed, as far as the timber was concerned, but the Indians not liking his words and manner, and disliking him on general principles, stopped cutting timber and cut Tom from his mule, continuing the chopping until, when his body was found later, it is said to have resembled something that had been run through a sausage grinder. It was one of the most thorough homicides ever pulled off, even in Indian Territory.

Mrs. Bailey, in the later 'eighties, married a man named Moore, the marriage being solemnized in her Rose Hill home. They lived together about a year, then Moore went back to Kansas and stayed. The Rose Hill house, like that in Paris, burned one night and Mrs. Moore afterwards lived on her Walnut Prairie farm until her death.

At Rose Hill, in the years following the war between the sections, were given some of the most lavish entertainments of those days. There were dances and dinners to which people from Texas, friends of the family, were invited, and showered with attention which left lasting memories.   [44]

In 1937 the Oklahoma Historical Society, under leadership of Judge, and former Oklahoma Governor, Robert L. Williams, secured the building by the WPA of a cobblestone fence around the burial ground at Rose Hill, where Colonel Jones and his first wife are buried. The fence, four and a half feet high and 330 feet around, is said to have cost $2,000. It is a fitting memorial of a remarkable man.

OUTLAWS VISITED THE VALLEY

"But for your petty, picking, downright thievery,
We scorn it as we do board wages."   —*Byron*

Tom Starr and Other Starrs
Jim Reed and Belle Reed Starr
John Middleton
Quantrell Was Here
Frank James Came Later

IN THE TEN YEARS previous to his death in Lamar County, in 1874, Jim Reed had committed an assortment of crimes that set a price on him, dead or alive. But for the fact that he was the first husband of the woman who became known as Belle Starr, he would have received little notice, and would have been forgotten long ago.

Reed and a companion named Morris were riding through the country, headed for Indian Territory, and stopped at the house of a farmer named Lowery in northwest Lamar County. They asked directions to get to Slate Shoals, a village in the extreme northeast corner of the County. Lowery directed them, and told them Slate Shoals was twenty-odd miles east of his place. It was late forenoon when the men rode away, and after going about three miles they stopped at the home of Charley Lee to get dinner.

Before going into the house Morris suggested that it would not look well for them to wear their pistols in the house where Mrs. Lee was preparing dinner, so they were hung over the saddle horns. Morris finished eating, saying he was not hungry, and went out of the house, returning almost immediately with his pistol in his hand, telling Reed to surrender, as he was an officer. Reed's reply was to upend the table, and with it in front of him he ran toward Morris, who shot him through the table top.

Reed lurched forward with the table and knocked Morris down. Though wounded, Reed appeared to be getting the best of the affair, having Morris under the table, when Lee grabbed Reed and pulled him back. The outlaw was so badly wounded that he died in a few minutes. Morris borrowed a wagon from Lee, put Reed's body in it, and accompanied by Lee and his wife took the body to Paris. There he showed credentials to an examining magistrate, who was told by Mrs. Lee the details of the

[49]

affair, and Morris was allowed to go. He bought a coffin from a Paris shop, put the body of Reed in it and next morning loaded it on the stage that ran from Paris to the end of the Texas and Pacific Rail Road at Brookston. Morris had told the examining magistrate that there was a reward of $1,000 for Reed, dead or alive; that he had gained Reed's confidence by pretending to be wanted by officers; and that they were on the way to Reed's headquarters in the Cherokee Nation. Where Morris took the body, who offered the reward, was never known by anyone in Paris. A story was current afterwards that Reed's wife was called to identify the body and that in order to prevent the killer getting the reward she denied the body was that of her husband. The story was told me by several persons who lived in Paris at the time.

A few days after Reed was killed a woman who told the Lees she was Reed's wife called at the Lee home and was told details of the killing. Thanking them, she left and they never heard of her again. Some years later Lowery was told that Morris had bought a small ranch west of Fort Worth, and that one morning he went out before daylight to feed his horses, and was shot and killed by an unknown person.

Belle Reed, before marriage, was Belle Shirley, daughter of a respectable Missouri family. She had two brothers who were members of Quantrell's guerillas. The younger of them, named Ed, was her twin. He joined Quantrell, where his older brother was serving. Frank Dalton, one of Quantrell's lieutenants, said Ed Shirley was killed when the Quantrell band met a company of Federal cavalry near Centralia, Missouri, in 1863.

Shirley was a Southern sympathizer, and presently his home was burned by the guerillas aligned with the North. The family decided to move to Texas, as did many other Missourians, and Shirley bought a small farm near Scyene, a Dallas County village. After the war ended a group of

[50]

young Missourians who had heard that unbranded cattle were plentiful in Texas, and were being taken up by anyone who wanted them, came to Texas and visited the Shirley family. Among them was Jim Reed, who had been a member with Ed Shirley of the Quantrell band. He said he knew the man who killed Ed, and Belle Shirley said she would marry the man who would kill the slayer of her brother. Reed left, and some time later came back, told Belle her brother was avenged, and she married him against the advice of her parents.

Reed was said to have started a livery stable in the town of Dallas, and was accused of buying and selling stolen horses. He left Dallas and later was joined by his wife, in California, where their son was born. They afterwards went back to the Cherokee Nation, and Reed put in with what was known as the Starr Gang.

Late in 1873 old Watt Grayson lived near North Fork in the Creek Nation. He was known to have a considerable sum of money, and a gang of robbers took him out of his home, put a rope around his neck, and pulled him up six times before he weakened and told them the money was buried under the hearth in the house. They took the money, about $30,000 in gold and silver coin, and got away with it. Jim Reed was one of the robbers, but the money was taken by old Tom Starr and was divided later. Reed found he was being trailed and went to Texas. He was on the way back to the Cherokee Nation when he was killed.

Another member of the gang was D. W. Wilder who was trailed into Texas, and with a man said to be another of the Grayson robbers, and a woman, were found by a posse in Bosque County, Texas. The three fought the officers, the woman making the biggest fight of all. Wilder was shot three times, then taken to Fort Smith. The other man got away and the woman was released as she was not concerned in the robbery of Watt Grayson.

[51]

After Reed was killed Belle went back to the Starrs and demanded Jim's share of the Grayson money. Old Tom refused to give any part of it to her and she then worked on his wife, but getting no consolation and no money she married Sam Starr, pet of the family, to spite Tom and his wife. They settled on Sam's land, near Briartown, in the Nation, and apparently intended to be good. Grayson died some time after the robbery and his heirs sued Tom Starr for the stolen money in Fort Smith Federal Court, but got none.

Introducing whisky into the Nation was an offense punishable by a penitentiary sentence, no matter how small the quantity. One night Sam and Belle were "throwing a party," deputy marshals raided the house and found some whisky. Sam and Belle were taken to Fort Smith, convicted and sentenced to serve short terms in House of Correction, Detroit, Michigan.

After they served their time and returned to the Cherokee Nation, Sam Starr and Felix Griffin were charged with robbing a small postoffice and were put under bond to appear for trial in Fort Smith. The case was continued and Belle, who had gone to Fort Smith to be a witness, started back home with the two men. On the way they found a dance in progress in a house and stopped there. Sam and one of the men at the dance began quarreling over Sam's charge that the other man had killed one of Sam's horses. Each drew his pistol and fired simultaneously, and both were killed.

Belle Starr lived with other husbands from time to time after Sam Starr's death. John Wyche, resident of Hugo, Oklahoma, told me of her death. John Wyche's grandmother was a sister of Tom Starr, and John had spent much time with the Starrs when a boy. He knew Belle and the others of the clan. He said that Belle was riding along a little-used road from Briartown to Eufaula, in 1889, when she was shot and killed. Her murderer was

[52]

never discovered, nor was the cause for the crime known.

Frank Dalton, an uncle of the Dalton brothers who for years terrorized parts of the West, robbing trains and banks, gave in his published reminiscences his version of Belle's death. He said Ed Reed, Belle's son, had become an outlaw in a small way and had served two brief terms in Federal prisons. In February, 1889, Ed was being sought by officers on a charge of robbing a store in Catoosa, in the Cherokee Nation. Dalton said Ed went to his mother's home and hid in the brush near it, waiting for night to go in and ask his mother for money. In the dusk he saw a man peering about in the yard and deciding the man was an officer searching for him, he fired, and killed Belle. She was dressed in men's clothes, as she usually did when at home, and was looking for a hole in the fence through which pigs had been getting into the field.

That is Dalton's story, but he did not say how he knew what Belle was doing when killed, nor did he say how he knew who killed her. The story sounds imaginary to me.

Newspapers in Indian Territory told of Ed Reed as a great outlaw, giving him some of his mother's reputation, but people who knew him said he was a small-time criminal. He was charged with stealing some cattle from an Indian, but evidence was that the Indian did not own a hoof and was a self-confessed perjurer, so Ed was released from Fort Smith jail. Later he was implicated in some minor violations of the laws, and agreed that if allowed to do so he would leave the Territory and never come back.

Belle Reed was in jail in Lamar County briefly not long before Jim Reed was killed. T. J. Vansant, who was born in Van Buren, Arkansas, and who when a small boy often saw old Tom Starr, came to Lamar County after serving in the Confederate Army. He settled in the southern part of the county and had a store near where now is the town of Ben Franklin. One morning in 1874 three men rode by the store in a hurry. Presently an officer rode up and

[53]

asked if anyone had passed. Vansant told him of the three men and the officer said one was Belle Starr who often wore men's clothing when out with her husband, Jim Reed. She was called Belle Starr even then, because of her association with that clan.

The officer had come from the vicinity of Dallas, trailing Reed, and Vansant and some others went with him in the direction the three riders had gone. They went nearly to Honey Grove, did not find the men, and started back. When near Roxton, Lamar County, they overtook a woman on horseback. She wore a riding skirt but Vansant recognized her as one of the three he had seen pass his store. She denied it, but finally admitted her identity and said she was trying to help her husband elude the officers. She was taken in charge and a local officer took her to Paris and she was put in jail, but was released after a day or two as there was no charge against her in Lamar County. It was about this time that Jim Reed was killed.

Belle Starr was a notorious figure in and about Fort Smith in the years after Sam Starr was killed. She took up with a Cherokee named Blue Duck and had their picture taken together. Blue was a member of the infamous Buck gang that preyed on the Nation a long time. He was hanged for murder after conviction in Fort Smith. Belle had another photograph that showed her sitting on a horse, wearing a riding skirt, a large tan felt hat with a red plume, and a pair of revolvers holstered at her waist. The photographer advertised copies of this picture for sale and did good business.

Henry Starr, a grandson of Tom, was held over in Lamar County jail a few days in 1896. He had been arrested for robbing a bank in Stroud, Oklahoma, and was being held for an order of transfer to Fort Smith. There he was convicted and sent to the penitentiary. Henry had been arrested when 18 years old, for horse theft. He was acquitted, and then was charged with introducing whisky,

[54]

but was set free in that case also. Then he started a career of real crime, covering Oklahoma, Arkansas, parts of Kansas and Colorado. He killed Deputy Marshal Wilson, was convicted in Fort Smith and sentenced to hang. Reversal gave him a new trial and he was sentenced to serve 18 years in prison. While waiting in Fort Smith jail to be sent to a Federal prison he persuaded Cherokee Bill to give him a pistol which had been smuggled in to him (Bill was under sentence of death at the time and was later hanged), and for this Henry was pardoned by President Theodore Roosevelt. He went into real estate business in Tulsa, Oklahoma, but learning that Arkansas was asking for his extradition to be tried for an old bank robbery in that state, he resumed his life of crime.

In 1921 Henry and three others tried to rob a bank in Harrison, Arkansas. The bank vault had a door in the rear. When the bandits put the bank employes in the vault the president, W. J. Myers, 63 years old, came out the rear door with a rifle and killed Starr.

One Lamar County man had some dealings with the Starrs and came out winner. Willie P. Francis was a stockman who also bred good horses back in the 'seventies and 'eighties of the last century. He had a little race mare he called Betty White. One Fall he put bows and a sheet in his wagon, tied Betty White behind, took his oldest son with him and went up into Missouri to make the rounds of the county fairs and races. On the way back to Texas he came to a good camping place in the Cherokee Nation and tied up for the night though it was rather early in the afternoon.

Charley Starr, a grandson of Tom, and some others came and seeing Betty White they recognized her as a race horse, and bantered Francis to match a race with a horse of theirs. There was a neighborhood track nearby and Francis accepted the challenge and agreed to stay over to next day to run the race.

[55]

The next morning old Tom Starr came to Francis' camp and said, "Stranger, I understand you have matched a race with the boys here, to be run this evening. My advice to you is to hitch up and move on. They know you have the better horse but they are going to take your money anyhow."

Francis told old Tom that he had never run out on an agreement to match a race and he was going to stay and run his mare. The race came off in due time, but the Starr gang had put a man wrapped in a white sheet near the end of the track. Betty White did not know about that sort of thing and she flew the track and the Starr horse won.

That night Charley Starr and some others went down to the Francis camp and suggested a game of poker. Poker was one of Francis' strong points, though Starr did not know that. Francis saw Charley stealing cards but as he was rather good at that himself he made no objection. Presently Charley had secured four kings and bet on his hand heavily. When the showdown came and Charley laid down the four kings and started to take the stakes, Francis laid down four aces. Charley took a look at them and said, "How in the hell did you get them four aces?" Francis replied, "I got them honest, just like you got your four kings." They gave Francis the money without protest.

Then Charley said to him, "You didn't come here to run horses, you came here to play poker. We don't need you any longer. You can hitch up in the morning and move on." Francis said that was advice he did not need as it was what he intended to do. After the Starr gang left Francis told his son he was afraid they might come back in the night and rob and murder him, so he told the boy what to do in case that happened. He was not disturbed during the night, however, and early next morning he was far on the road to Texas.

The next Spring Francis got a letter from Charley

[56]

Starr, saying he had been elected a member of the Cherokee Council which was to meet soon in Tahlequah. Starr's letter told how many members the Council had and said their pay was five dollars a day and they would be in session ninety days. He said every one of the members played poker and that if Francis would come up there and go partners with him they would have all the money at the close of the session, and added, "If you don't believe what I say, just write me that you will come and I will send you the money to pay your expenses."

Francis answered the letter and told Charley Starr he did not want to have anything more to do with him, and added, "If I were to come up there and help you win their money, you would take it from me before I could get away."

[Francis told this story to M. F. Drummond, in Drummond's store in Brookston, Texas, where Mr. Drummond made a note of it and years later told it to me.]

JOHN MIDDLETON was a Lamar County youth who was mixed up with the Starr gang for a time. He began in a small way, as did many of the "bad men" of the West. In 1879 he and his half-brother, Jap, went to the house of a family named Chance, one of the sons being a friend, and they asked Mrs. Chance to lend them her scissors to give each other a "foxy" hair cut. She refused, for fear they might break her scissors, so the youths went to the barn, got a pair of sheep shears and cut each others' hair. While one youth's hair was being cut he would bleat like a sheep. While John's hair was being cut the shears slipped and a slice was taken off the top of one ear, and John remarked that the shears were too sharp.

Soon after this John and Jap committed their first theft, so far as was known. They took from a man in Walden, Arkansas, some shoes, a pair of boots, some pocket knives and some garden seed. Both youths were drunk and going

[57]

home they again stopped at the Chance home and John gave Mrs. Chance some seed, saying he had bought more than he needed, and gave her son a pocket knife. Officers from Arkansas followed them and a friend of the Middletons warned them they were being looked for. Jap surrendered but John got on his horse and left for Indian Territory and was not caught. Jap was released for it appeared he had no part in the stealing in Arkansas.

The Chance family moved to Cherokee Nation and one day John Middleton visited them. A man who had married one of the daughters of the Chance family had a fight with a man Middleton knew and disliked. John offered to bring in the fellow's scalp by sunup, or "maybe an hour by sun," but the Chance son-in-law said he didn't want the man killed. Middleton changed his clothes, shaved and left.

In the northeast corner of Lamar County, Red River runs over a rock formation, known as Slate Shoals. At ordinary stages the river can be forded there. It was a crossing place for horse thieves who stole horses in Missouri and Indian Territory and brought them to Texas to sell, or stole in Texas and took them north by the same route.

Late one day in the early 'eighties a farmer noticing the fence was down in a place where it fenced out a thicket, went in the maze of underbrush and bushes and saw two horses tied to a bush. He did not know the horses and left them tied. Presently four men riding, coming apparently from Indian Territory and carrying shot guns, rode by the farmer's house and into the thicket. It was about dark and shots were heard but the men were seen no more. Next morning some men went to the place and found a dead man, the horses gone. The body was brought out and viewed by the justice of the peace and was identified by a man who lived in the Territory as Dave Bowen, who also lived in the Territory and was known to have been

[58]

associating with Middleton. Slate Shoals folks refused to let the dead man be buried in the graveyard so a rude box was made, a woman gave a sheet to wrap the body, and he was buried beside the road.

Not long afterwards John Middleton was arrested by Lamar County officers and put in jail, charged with bringing stolen property in the form of horses into Texas. He became ill and by advice of the county jail physican was put in a room of the jailer's residence which was a part of the jail building. He was apparently so ill that close watch was not kept on him, and one night in 1884 he disappeared. Search was made for him but officers never found him.

John Milsap, who had been a Lamar County officer, became interested in the case, and decided John had gone back to Indian Territory to his old haunts, which were then comparatively safe from officers and a refuge for criminals of every sort. Milsap rode over much of eastern Indian Territory and presently heard that a man who tried to cross Poteau River south of Fort Smith, when the water was high, had been drowned, and that some Indians had found the body and buried it near the river.

The meager description of this drowned man led Milsap to believe it might be Middleton. He got one of the Indians who had helped at the burial to guide him to the place and they dug up the body, which was by then badly decomposed. Milsap took off a piece of the cloth of the man's coat, which was of a distinct and unusual pattern or weave, and reburied the remains. He then went to see Belle Starr, who had been a friend of Middleton, and showed her the piece of cloth. Belle said it was like the pattern of the coat John Middleton wore when last she saw him, not long before the drowning.

Belle was then at liberty on bond to appear at Fort Smith Court and answer a charge of being an accomplice of Middleton in stealing a horse from a man named

[59]

McCarthy, a resident of the Territory, after Middleton had escaped from Lamar County jail. It was this horse the drowned man had been riding. Identification of the cloth and the horse led Milsap to believe that he had found Middleton, but too late, and that Middleton had paid with his life instead of a probable penitentiary sentence in Texas.

WILLIAM QUANTRELL visited the Red River Valley, once, certainly, and more than once according to rather nebulous stories. The certain time was in the Fall of 1863 and the place was Sherman. The Reverend John H. McLean, who was a Methodist minister, stationed in Sherman that year, wrote in his reminiscences about fifty years later: "The day I was leaving Sherman to attend conference in Jefferson, Quantrell and his men arrived in Sherman and stopped on Travis street, in front of a little brick office I had been occupying. They were very quiet and civil in appearance. Quantrell was pointed out to me. He had a refined and civil look and was dubbed 'parson' by some of his men. He was said to have been at one time a school teacher but because of certain outrages committed by Kansas Jayhawkers on the Quantrell family in Missouri, he became desperate and showed no quarter to such foes. This was told me by one who was a near neighbor of the Quantrells in Missouri at the time the offenses were committed. One of Quantrell's captains married a Sherman young lady of a prominent family and he was later killed in guerilla warfare."

A moving picture shown in Bonham, Texas, about ten years ago was said to have mentioned the name of a Fannin County family in connection with the Dalton boys, who were the subjects of the picture. Then oldtimers began to recall that the Daltons who held forth muchly in Indian Territory also visited Fannin County at times though they were not charged with engaging in their brand of business

[60]

while there. The story said, and being told by reputable people was entitled to credence, that Fannin County also entertained Frank and Jesse James and that more famous guerilla, William Quantrell, and more than once.

Quantrell once camped south of Bonham, the story said, and coming into town one day and feeling frisky, he and his men rode around the courthouse and as they rode Quantrell drew his six-shooter and began to fire at the arrow that served as a wind vane on the cupola of the courthouse. He then said that if there was a hole in the feathered end of the arrow he made it. Otherwise he would not admit having shot at the arrow. Years passed. The commissioners decided the old court house was likely to fall down and maybe hurt somebody, so they would build a new one. When the arrow was removed during the wrecking of the old building there was a hole through the feathered end of the arrow, and it was plainly not a hole made by a woodpecker. The tale is not improbable but lacks documentary backing and may be taken for what it is worth.

Frank Dalton, uncle of the Daltons who robbed banks, said Quantrell's real name was Charley Hart. He said, as Mr. McLean did, that Charley had been a school teacher, and that he became a guerilla officer after being whipped in Lawrence, Kansas, in 1862, because he would not take the oath of allegiance to the United States, and was then ordered to leave Lawrence. He did leave, went to Missouri, and began his reprisals against the people who had mistreated him.

There is no record, nor even tradition that both James brothers were ever in Lamar County, but there is no doubt that one of them, Frank James, the elder of the brothers, was briefly in Lamar County after Jesse James had been killed and Frank had been pardoned by the Governor of Missouri. Frank was employed by A. G. Hubbard, a dry goods and men's clothing merchant in Paris in the 'eighties

[*61*]

of the last century. It was said that he also had been similarly employed by Sanger Brothers in Dallas. He was supposed to be a sort of a floor-walker or greeter, but would act as a salesman at times if the volume of business required. He attracted some patronage, to be sure, for a youth who could say, "I bought this shirt from Frank James" had a sort of brief prominence among his fellows.

I saw Frank James many times while he was employed in the clothing store. He seemed to be a quiet, self-possessed man, with no sign, at least to me, of having been an outlaw.

Frank James died in his bed on the old home place, the Samuels farm, near Kearney, Missouri, in February, 1915. A funeral gathering was addressed by Judge John Phillips, who 33 years before had defended Frank in Gallatin, and secured acquittal, the last case Missouri held against Frank. The casket was sent to St. Louis, the body cremated and the ashes put in an urn and sent to Kansas City and placed in a burial vault.

TWO PAID THE PENALTY

"And naked to the hangman's noose
The morning clocks will ring;
A neck God made for other use
Than strangling in a string."
            —*A. E. Housman*

Execution of Lovett Cady

IN 1854 Pine Bluffs was a village near the bank of Red River, northwest of Clarksville. Among other establishments there were two groggeries, as places where whisky was sold then were called. One was kept by Sam Sinclair, the other by Lovett Cady. They were competitors in business. One day in September, 1854, Cady poked his rifle out of a window in his place and shot Sinclair who was standing in the door of his place. He was arrested, put in jail in Clarksville and in December the grand jury indicted him and two others. George Frazier, charged with complicity in the homicide, was tried immediately and acquitted, whereupon Cady asked and was given a continuance until the Spring term of Court. Ten days later Miller Husbands, the other man charged as an accomplice, was tried and acquitted.

At the June, 1855, term of Court, Cady was put on trial and a verdict of first degree murder was returned by the jury ten minutes after it retired to consider the evidence. Cady had offered no evidence in his own defense. He had stated under oath that he had been assaulted and beaten by three men, friends of Sinclair, and that he had not dared to go outside of his own house for three months. He was apparently unable to substantiate this, at least he did not do so. The trial and verdict was on a Wednesday and on Friday Judge W. S. Todd sentenced Cady to be hanged on Friday, June 29, and called his attention to the fact that he had granted him 21 days of life—far more than Cady gave the man he murdered.

Judge Todd's language in sentencing Cady, is worthy of preservation in addition to the records of Red River County. He said:

[65]

"Lovett Cady, charged by the State with the crime of murder, you have been arraigned before a Jury of your peers and after argument of counsel and a careful dispassionate examination of all the witnesses, you stand convicted according to the law and the evidence. It now becomes my painful duty to pronounce the sentence of the law against you for the shedding of innocent blood.

"The crime of murder is one of awful malignity in the sight of God and of man, even when perpetrated on an enemy and under ordinary circumstances. How much more then, in your case, when you have in cold blood and without apparent provocation taken the life of an unoffending man. If, in the midst of a sudden passion which sometimes overtakes the wisest and the best, you had dealt the fatal blow, your guilt might have been somewhat extenuated; but you deliberately planned the murder and as artfully sought to hide it after it was consummated.

"You laid your plans in secret—you conspired against the life of Samuel Sinclair, your nearest neighbor, and you executed your hellish purpose under cover of your own roof. You ushered his soul into eternity by shooting a bullet through his body while he stood, an unsuspecting victim, within the door of his own domicile, enjoying, as he had a right to suppose, that security and immunity from harm which a man's house, or his castle as the law regards it, seldom fails in a Christian country.

"Your heart seemed steeped in depravity and totally bent upon mischief. You must, therefore, feel the justice of the sentence about to be pronounced on you, for although you are represented to be poor, and in social position not high, you have had the highest privileges which the Law affords to any citizen. You have had the benefit of able counsel who have faithfully performed their duty towards you—a jury of twelve impartial freemen, entertaining no prejudice against you but selected by yourself and sworn to do you justice. By these you have been pro-

[66]

nounced guilty of murder, so cowardly and cruel as to leave no doubt upon my mind as to your guilt.

"In granting you twenty-one days respite I extend to you far more mercy than you showed your victim. You gave him no time to make his peace with God. To you I grant all these privileges and I earnestly recommend you to set about preparing for the awful moment when you will have to meet your victim at a higher Bar than this and account to your God for the blood you have shed which, like Abel's, cries from the ground.

"Lovett Cady, you have my deepest sympathy, not that you have to suffer the punishment of the law, for that is just—but that you should have been so depraved, so lost to virtue and to every manly feeling of compassion, as to lift your hand to shed the blood of a brother man. I admonish you, therefore, as your fellow mortal, bound to account for all my acts, that you will humble your heart for your horrible crime. There is no pardon here for you except the Executive clemency, and it would be more than folly for you to indulge in such a hope. God, however, is an all-merciful as well as all-powerful being and able, though your sins be as scarlet, to make you white as snow.

"My sentence is, therefore, that on Friday, the 29th day of the present month, you be taken from the jail by the sheriff of the county between the hours of 9 o'clock a. m. and 4 o'clock p. m., and be hung by the neck until you are dead, and may God have mercy on your soul."

After Judge Todd concluded, Cady said, "I confess that I killed Sam Sinclair, but I was compelled to do so to save my own life. I was shut up in my own house and afraid to leave it. I had been assaulted, beaten and left for dead by the bandit crew who, finding they had not killed me, was determined to have my life anyhow. Three guns were kept loaded for three months to kill me and for no other reason than that I kept an opposition house. I can prove this. My case has not been rightly handled, or I would not now be

[67]

under this sentence. Before God and this Court, this is true. I appeal to anyone who has known me from my infancy, if I was ever inclined to injure any man unless compelled to do it. Before God and this Court, this is true."

Clarksville Standard, reporting the verdict, said, "We are told that the prisoner listened to the sentence without evincing emotion, but his wife who was present and, as has been supposed, instigated the murder, was very much affected though, as one would suppose, as we are told, that from looking at the two she was the least likely to be troubled by any of the softer emotions. Cady is a small, thin-faced man, about 50 years of age; his wife a stout woman of threatening manner and coarse expression, perhaps 40 years of age. They have, we believe, two daughters."

The Standard's issue the week following June 29, 1855, said, "About 3 o'clock Cady was hung, about two miles north of town in the Round Grove. He deported himself under the scaffold with a gravity and propriety becoming his situation, participated in prayer and avowed religious convictions and hopes. The Reverend J. W. P. McKenzie ministered him and expressed the hope his two daughters would never be held accountable for the act of their father. His wife attended him to the scaffold and stayed with him to the last. She shrieked as the halter was adjusted to his neck and when he swung off she ran to him and endeavored to hold him up until Sheriff West removed her. Driving the cart from under him allowed him to fall about three inches. Pulsation of the arteries was perceptible for about twenty minutes, but there was little struggle. After hanging 35 minutes he was taken down and found still warm, so much so that his wife for a little time entertained a belief that he might be restored."

The Clue of the Broken Fence Picket

NEAR FORTY YEARS before Arthur Koehler matched the ends of two boards to make an unbreakable link in the chain of evidence which convicted Bruno Hauptmann of the murder of the Lindbergh baby; before Police Commissioner Lewis Valentine's plainclothes men used a piece of upholsterers' twine to send John Fierenzo to the electric chair for killing Nancy Titterton, a Texas sheriff, who wore broad-brimmed hats and high-heeled boots, who knew nothing of psychology and laboratory practice, but who was familiar with human nature and the everyday customs of his people, matched the broken pieces of a fence picket, and eighteen months later hanged the man who had committed a murder, the hunt for whom had started with the clue of the broken fence picket.

November 13, 1897, the hands going to work on the farm of J. J. Roach, near Celeste, a town in Hunt County, Texas, saw that a house of two rooms, which had long been vacant, had burned in the night. Among the hands was a young man who entertained himself by playing a fiddle. Since Roach objected to the noise, the young man kept his fiddle in the old house and played it there when at leisure. He realized his fiddle was destroyed, but poked around in the ruins and found what he thought was the neck of his fiddle. Picking it up he saw it was a human bone, and it proved to be a wrist bone. The remainder of a body was found, lying on its back and charred beyond recognition.

Sheriff Max Patton was notified and a justice of the peace held an inquest, finding that the then unidentified man was apparently murdered by some person unknown. A piece of the man's coat under his body was not entirely burned and by the pattern it was later identified as having been worn by Ben Stonecypher.

[69]

Sheriff Patton began looking for something that might give him a lead in his search for the person who committed the crime, for he was convinced the man had been killed and robbed as there were none of the personal belongings that would have been found had the man died by accident. He saw wheel tracks in the seldom used road near the burned house, the width showing they were made by a buggy, but there was nothing to show from or to where it was driven nor by whom.

That part of the Roach farm was fenced in a manner then common in Texas. Pickets, roughly split from bois d'arc (called osage orange in northern states, a very hard and durable wood) were laced together with wire and nailed to posts. The sheriff observed that the top of one of the pickets, where wheel prints and horse tracks showed a horse and buggy had stood near the fence, was broken off close to the top wire and a strand of the wire had been twisted off. The break was not weathered and therefore had been made recently. Knowing the method of temporary mending of vehicles in use at that time, the sheriff was convinced that the person who had driven the buggy away from the place had a vehicle with a cracked or broken shaft, which he had mended by binding the piece of bois d'arc around the break with the wire.

His task then was to find that buggy and the person who had driven it.

For ten days the sheriff and other officers went from house to house and village to village in Hunt County, looking for and asking about a buggy with a shaft wired with a piece of bois d'arc, and at last it was located. At a livery barn in Wolfe City, a town north of Greenville, the county seat, a man had left a buggy early in the morning of November 13, with instructions to have a new pair of shafts fitted to it. This had been done and the man had called for the buggy and driven it off, leaving the broken shafts at the livery barn. The barn owner said the man gave his name as Charlie Little, but this was not proof that he had committed a murder.

Sheriff Patton took the piece of bois d'arc from the broken buggy shaft, went back to where the house burned, and the piece exactly fitted the broken picket on the fence. Then he was sure the driver of the buggy had been at the place and was probably the murderer. Now he knew for whom he was looking.

Charlie Little, a farm laborer, was not yet thirty years old. He was married and had two daughters, five and six years old. Ben Stonecypher, the victim, was about the same age, not married and having no relatives in Texas so far as appeared. He was a barber, but picking cotton in the Fall was sometimes more profitable than following his trade in a country town, and he and Little had been working together several weeks on farms near Wolfe City in October and November.

Little had not been at home since the night the house had burned, and Sheriff Patton, former Sheriff Jeff Mason and Constable Myrick of Wolfe City learned from people who had seen them that Little and a young man, John Woodard, had driven in a buggy through Ladonia and Honey Grove in Fannin County, north of Hunt County, nearly east through Paris and on to Clarksville in Red River County, nearly a hundred miles from Greenville. Going to Clarksville they were joined by Sheriff Seth Dinwiddie of Red River County, and tracing back toward Paris they located Little on a farm in the eastern part of Lamar County, where he and Woodard were picking cotton.

Not knowing how much trouble they might have in making the arrest, the officers surrounded the house before daylight. In the early morning of November 23, Little, who was known by Sheriff Patton, came out and picked up a stick of firewood. Patton came up behind Little, ordered him to raise his hands and told him he was under arrest for the murder of Ben Stonecypher, having in the meantime learned the identity of the dead man. Little replied, "I did it in self defense," and made no other statement at the time.

The Hunt County grand jury was in session at the time, and to forestall possible trouble in getting Little back to Greenville without having a warrant for his arrest, Patton had wired his office a day or two before, asking that an indictment be returned. This was done and the warrant was then in the hands of the office deputy. Little made no demur at going back, however, and asked that Woodard, the young man accompanying him, be released, declaring Woodard had nothing to do with the crime, and in fact knew nothing of it. This proved true and Woodard was released after the return to Greenville.

Little was brought to trial in Greenville before Judge Howard Templeton at the Spring Term of Court, 1898. Three days were used hearing testimony and arguments, Little having pleaded not guilty. April 27 the jury returned a verdict of murder in the first degree and assessed the death penalty. An appeal was taken and in November the Court of Appeals affirmed the judgment, but as District Court was not then in session in Hunt County it was March 10, 1899, that Little was brought before the Court for sentence. "Having nothing to say in bar thereof" as the record states, he was sentenced to hang on April 13. An appeal to Governor Joe Sayers resulted in two respites to allow the Governor time to study the record and evidence, the last ending May 4. The Governor having notified the sheriff he would not commute the sentence to life imprisonment the execution took place, inside the Hunt County jail.

A few days before the execution Little wrote and gave his spiritual adviser what he declared was a true statement of the affair. He said he and Stonecypher were going to see "some women" who lived near Leonard, another vil-

[72]

lage, in Fannin County. Finding the women were not at home they came back toward Celeste in Little's buggy. They had been drinking and stopped at the old house when Stonecypher suggested that they play cards. They sat on the porch and after a while he found Stonecypher was cheating, and so he reached for the pot, a few dollars. Stonecypher grabbed a shot gun that Little kept in his buggy, and which had been brought on the porch. When Little refused to relinquish the pot, Stonecypher hit him on the head with the gun, Little picked up a piece of an old cultivator lying on the porch and hit Stonecypher, who fell back and did not answer when spoken to. Finding the man was dead, Little said he left the place in his buggy, after mending the break in the shaft which he had not noticed until then, and went to his home; thought of going to the sheriff and surrendering but changed his mind, started off in his buggy, picked up Woodard and they drove to Red River County and resumed cotton picking. He said he did not fire the house and that it must have caught fire from the lighted candle they were using for light in playing cards. He concluded the statement by warning young men against whisky, gambling, and bad company and professed peace with his Maker.

Testimony for the State was that Stonecypher had told other friends he was going to Southern Texas to be married and Little volunteered to take him to the railroad at Wolfe City. Stonecypher had over $100 in cash and some small change, as was shown when they paid for lunch at Celeste. As it was some time before a train was due on which Stonecypher could go south they started to call on the women and stopped at the old house to play cards.

Physical evidence was that Stonecypher's body was not found where the porch had been but inside the house; that the piece of iron was not by the body but was found in a dry cistern at the rear of the house, with hair and threads of raw cotton sticking to it; that the back of the man's head

[73]

was crushed and not the front as would have been the case if he was struck as Little declared.

Other evidence showed Little was in Wolfe City the day following the fire, had his buggy washed and new shafts attached; that he bought a good suit of clothes, some jewelry and a pearl-handled pen. He exchanged a watch, proved to have belonged to Stonecypher, at a Wolfe City jewelry store, paying $6 additional. That he went to the Merrell farm where Stonecypher had last picked cotton, asked for Stonecypher's trunk, stating the latter had gone to South Texas and wanted the trunk sent by express. It was shipped to Galveston from where it was returned by request of Sheriff Patton.

Sheriff Max Patton was well acquainted with Little before the crime and considered him a good friend. Before he was executed, and after he had abandoned all hope of a commutation, Little told the sheriff that he had not intended to kill Stonecypher but that he did expect to take his money and that was his purpose when he proposed the game. Finding the man was dead he fired the house, hoping to conceal the crime by destruction of the body.

The broken fence picket started the chain of evidence that put the rope around his neck.

————

MAX PATTON was born in Lamar County, Texas, son of R. J. Patton who had been a county commissioner in Reconstruction days and who was "removed" by the military authority because he and two other commissioners refused to include Negroes on the jury lists they were required to draw. Max Patton became deputy sheriff in Hunt County, then was elected sheriff and served several terms. In later years he was a special agent for the Texas Midland Railroad, settling claims and ferreting out robberies of cars. He passed away in Greenville several years ago.

THE PARIS FEDERAL COURT

Judge David E. Bryant

"It doth appear you are a worthy judge;
You know the law; your exposition
Hath been most sound."—Shakespeare

The Hay Meadow Massacre

"Murder most foul, as in the best it is;
But this most foul . . ."—Shakespeare

The Deputy U.S. Marshals

"Courage consists not in hazarding without
fear, but being resolutely minded in a
just cause."   *—Plutarch*

SQUARE-SHOULDERED and soldierly erect, a brown-bearded man walked into the Federal Court room in Paris, Texas. The people who had assembled there rose to their feet, the Court crier intoned:

"Hear ye, Hear ye, the Honorable Circuit and District Court for the Eastern District of Texas is now in session. All who have business with this Court approach and be heard. God save the United States and this Honorable Court"—

and David E. Bryant took his seat on the bench of a Court over which he was to preside twenty years. In the first ten years of that tenure there passed before him a parade of criminals of every degree—murderers, robbers, horse thieves, cattle and hog stealers, whisky peddlers and what-nots, each getting justice in fullest measure that Judge Bryant could dispense.

The Paris Division of the Court was established by an act of the Congress to relieve the Fort Smith Court of part of its heavy burden, in a jurisdiction that included all of Indian Territory and Oklahoma Territory. It left the Fort Smith Court the Cherokee, Creek, Osage and some smaller tribes in the northeast part of Indian Territory and gave Paris the Choctaw and Chickasaw Nations and all that wide expanse in the west that was Oklahoma Territory. The Eastern Texas District included 55 Texas counties, from Galveston to Paris, besides the Oklahoma and Indian Territories area.

The first term of the Paris Court was held April 29, 1889. Judge L. S. Sabin, who had presided over the District some years, was ill, and this first session was presided over by Judge Alex. Boarman of Shreveport, Louisiana. Dick Reagan, brother of U. S. Senator John H. Reagan, was marshal, nearing the end of his term. John E. McComb was district attorney.

[77]

There were few cases to be tried, most of them civil actions. The grand jury returned 24 indictments, 12 for liquor violations, the others for murder and assorted crimes. In explanation of the small number of bills the grand jury told Judge Boarman that "The extensiveness of the territory and the impossibility of having speedy access to many parts of it have made it impossible for us to complete investigation of many cases, and we regret to say that there remains a vast amount of work that could not be completed in the limited time we have been permitted to sit."

That condition did not last long. Judge Sabin died, Judge Bryant was named to succeed him, and J. J. Dickerson was made marshal at the end of Reagan's term. Marshal Dickerson had under him sometimes as many as eighty deputies, men who rode the territory and brought in criminals almost daily, summoned witnesses and jurors, and risked their lives time and again, sometimes losing them.

Within six months after taking the oath, Judge Bryant presided at the trial of twelve men charged with murder, six of them being convicted. This was the famous case of the United States vs. C. E. Cook et al., generally known as the Hay Meadow Massacre, when four men were killed and a fifth one was left for dead in the Neutral Strip—No Man's Land—between Texas and Kansas. The verdict was reversed by Supreme Court of United States, and the Department of Justice decided not to have another trial. It was believed that the witnesses, who had scattered to the four quarters of the country, could not be again assembled, and some of them were dead beyond recall.

That was the first of many trials for murder before Judge Bryant, which resulted in conviction and sentence of more than a dozen, nine of whom were hanged in Lamar County jail yard at various times, singly or in groups, the others being given commutations by the President. It was a busy ten years, then jurisdiction of the Paris and Fort Smith Courts over Indian Territory and Oklahoma Territory was given to courts that sat in the two territories.

Something of the magnitude of the work Judge Bryant did may be seen by the record of one term. In the November, 1892, term he found 176 cases ready for setting on the docket—27 for murder, the same number for assault to kill, others for adultery, polygamy (the Federal name for bigamy), counterfeiting, horse theft, perjury, robbery, theft from U. S. mails, receiving stolen property, assault to rob, making false claim against the government, and many cases of introducing liquor or selling liquor in Indian Territory. One of the men convicted of murder was later hanged. Other murder cases were either continued to another term of court or the charge was reduced to manslaughter because of extenuating circumstances, and some were acquitted. The docket was cleared, for Judge Bryant allowed no waste of time. When he was on the bench the United States of America was holding Court, and it was held in conformity to his belief in our country and its greatness.

Judge Bryant had a sense of humor that was shown at times. One day he was sentencing some bootleggers, who were called whisky peddlers in Indian Territory. I once heard him ask one how much he had sold, and the fellow replied, "Three quarts and a pint." Judge Bryant said, "You know, if I was in the whisky selling business in that country, I'd sell enough to make it worth while. I wouldn't go to the penitentiary for selling quarts; I'd sell barrels. I'll give you a year and a day in the penitentiary." That was the minimum sentence. At another time he advised a peddler that the only safe way to introduce whisky into the Territory was to drink it before crossing the border.

One Indian was tried twice and sentenced for repeating an offense. Levi Shelt, a Cherokee Indian, had married a girl when he and she attended school. After living together

[79]

several years he left her and "took up" with another woman, and was tried and sentenced for adultery. After finishing the sentence he returned to the same woman and again was tried and convicted. When Judge Bryant asked him, as he usually did, if he had anything to say why he should not be sentenced, Shelt replied, "Nothing, except that I am not guilty."

Judge Bryant asked, "Levi, did I not send you to the penitentiary for adultery?" and Levi replied that he had. "For how long?" the Judge asked, "For a year and a day," Levi replied. "And when you were released you came back and did the same thing?" Judge Bryant asked, and again the reply was "Yes." Then the Judge asked why he did it and Levi said simply, "I loved the woman, sir." The Judge studied a moment, then sentenced Levi to serve fifteen months at hard labor in Detroit House of Correction, and turned to the next case.

One day when I was in the court room a Negro man was on trial for polygamy. Testimony showed he had married in Red River County, Texas, had left, and gone to Indian Territory and married another woman without having been divorced in Texas. On the jury that tried him was a man who kept a boarding house in Paris, who had come from Red River County, where he had been a justice of the peace in a country precinct.

The Negro offered in his defense that he had been divorced, but District Court in Red River County had no record of it. Finally Judge Bryant took a hand himself, as he sometimes did when he wanted to get at the heart of a matter without waste of words. He asked the Negro how he got his divorce. The Negro said Squire White gave it to him. When asked where the Squire could be found, the Negro said, pointing to the jury box, "Dar he sets, right over dar." It developed that the Squire had married the Negroes, and when trouble arose and the man asked about a divorce he concluded that as he had married them he could

[80]

divorce them, and did so. The Negro believed he was divorced and the jury acquitted him.

Judge Bryant could be stern when he felt it was called for, yet when stern he was fair. One instance was when a young man charged with murder was tried and the jury returned a verdict of manslaughter. Sentences were not fixed by the jury. They only returned the verdict and the Judge fixed sentence, limited only by the provisions of the law. Sentence was usually not pronounced immediately after the verdict was returned, but toward the end of the week when the Judge had taken time to consider the case.

In this instance he told the convicted man to stand and asked him if he had anything to say why sentence should not be pronounced. The reply was that he hoped the Judge would be as lenient as possible. Judge Bryant said, "You were charged with murder. The evidence, to my mind, was conclusive of that crime, but the jury took a different view, and decided your crime was manslaughter. How they arrived at that verdict is beyond my comprehension, but that is their verdict. The law allows me to give you no more than ten years in the penitentiary. I will give you that. Have your seat."

In January, 1896, the body of Lee Crum, a young white man, was found near Kiamichi River above Antlers, I. T. His ears had been cut off, his eyes gouged out and his face slashed. Clues led to arrest of an Indian youth who told deputy marshals that he and two others had shot Crum, who was badly wounded but did not die at once. Next morning they returned to the place, finished killing and disfiguring Crum, hoping he would not be identified. One boy was 13 years old, the others a year or two older.

They were brought to Paris for trial before Judge Bryant. Evidence, in addition to the confession, was conclusive as to two of them and they were sentenced to the penitentiary for life, because on account of their age they could not be hanged. They were sent to the Ohio State

[81]

Penitentiary in Columbus, and a year later the 13-year-old boy died and was buried in the prison cemetery. So juvenile delinquency is not new.

There is no "unwritten law" in Federal Courts, even in the South, where such a plea usually gets acquittal for a homicide committed on one alleged to have wronged or insulted a female relative of the killer. Fortunately for a Texas man who was tried before Judge Bryant in April, 1900, he had self defense as a plea and proved it. The man's hired hand had enticed his wife to run away with him, taking the youngest child of the couple with her. They went from Texas into Indian Territory and the husband went after the child, concluding to let the wife go her way. The woman urged the hired man to kill her husband, and he said he would. This was told the husband by people who heard the woman's demand.

When the husband got the child he started back to Texas and the two men met on the road, each riding a horse. The husband got off his horse and as he was dismounting the hired man ran at him with an open knife. The husband turned, drew his pistol and shot and killed the hired man. There was ample proof and an acquittal.

Judge David E. Bryant was a great-grandson of Anthony Bryant, a Virginian, descendant of an English family. Anthony Bryant had a son, David, born in Buckingham County, Virginia, who was taken by his parents to Kentucky when a child. When he was grown to manhood he married and was a planter. This David Bryant had a son, A. M. Bryant, born in 1818, and reared to manhood in Greene County, Kentucky, where he married Clarissa Young, daughter of a pioneer family. In 1853 they came to Grayson County, Texas, with their two children, Maria and David.

In Grayson County A. M. Bryant bought 420 acres of land, which was added to from time to time, until he owned a thousand acres of the best farm land in the county.

[82]

He was County Judge of Grayson County after the war between the sections, and was a member of the Convention that drafted the Texas Constitution during the reconstruction.

The daughter died when a child, but David grew to manhood and was destined for the legal profession. He graduated from Trinity College, North Carolina, in 1871, with the B. A. degree, returned to Sherman, Texas, and was admitted to the bar the next year. Five years later he formed a partnership with Tom Brown, one of Texas' ablest lawyers, and when this terminated after about six years David Bryant took Frank Dillard as a law practice partner.

In 1876 David Bryant married a daughter of Judge J. B. Thompson, of Preston, Grayson County. Judge Bryant passed away in 1910, in a hospital in St. Louis, where he had gone for treament of a chronic ailment. He was succeeded by Gordon Russell, a Texas Democratic Congressman, appointed by President Taft, and after his death W. L. Estes was appointed by President Wilson.

After Judge Estes passed away, David Bryant's son, Randolph Bryant, who had been Federal District Attorney for several years, was named to the vacancy. He has the judicial example of his father and his grand-father as his guide in presiding over the Federal Court of Eastern District of Texas.

The Hay Meadow Massacre

JUNE 10, 1890, twelve men sat in the prisoner's dock in the Federal Court in Paris, Texas, and faced the twelve jurors who were to decide if they were guilty of the murder of John M. Cross, July 25, 1888, in the "Neutral Strip" commonly referred to as No Man's Land, between Kansas and Oklahoma. The jury, composed of citizens of Fannin and Red River Counties, heard the testimony and argu-

[83]

ments of counsel until 6 o'clock the evening of July 5, and on Tuesday, July 8, returned its verdict, finding six of the men guilty as charged, five not guilty, and mistrial as to one who had become ill during the trial and in whose case a mistrial had been agreed on.

Judge David E. Bryant sentenced the six found guilty to be hanged December 19, 1890, execution by hanging being mandatory under Federal law at that time, and which could be stayed only by the President granting commutation. An appeal was taken to the United States Supreme Court, and on March 6, 1891, the mandate of the Supreme Court was received, reversing the case because of error, and the men were released. They were never tried again, as it was deemed impossible to get the witnesses, who had scattered over the country, and the expense of the trial was enormous, $115,000 having been spent paying witnesses, jurors and other necessary costs in the first trial.

The killing of John M. Cross, sheriff of Stevens County, Kansas, and his posse, Robert Hubbard, R. T. Wilcox and C. W. Eaton and the wounding of Herbert Tonney in No Man's Land on the night of July 25, 1888, was a crime almost without a parallel in the civilized world. The incidents leading up to and connected with that bloody tragedy read like a story of border life.

The troubles in Stevens county, Kansas, which culminated in the killing, began with the temporary organization of the county in 1886, which was done by the proclamation of Governor Martin, of Kansas. Hugoton was designated as the county seat. The governor appointed J. W. Calvert county clerk, and J. B. Chamberlain, J. B. Robertson and W. A. Clark county commissioners, who were all residents of the southern portion of the county.

In order to permanently organize the county, it was necessary to have a population of 2500. The county commissioners had a census taken. This showed that the county contained 2662 persons. The people of Woodsdale and the northern portion of the county denounced it as a fraud, and under the leadership of Colonel Sam Wood, founder of Woodsdale, proceeded to take evidence to show that it was not correct. However, the election was ordered by the county commissioners and notices were posted. When the election came off the people of Woodsdale and the northern portion of the county refrained from voting. The result was that Hugoton was almost unanimously selected as the county seat. It was contested in the courts and the election set aside, thus continuing the temporary organization.

During the campaign for the county seat election Colonel Sam Wood, whose home was at that time in Topeka, was in Stevens county actively engaged in securing evidence to show that the census was fraudulent. A few days after the election, in company with Captain I. C. Price, an attorney of Woodsdale, he started to Garden City, Kansas, to take the train for Topeka to file notice of a contest in the county seat election, when they were kidnaped. They were taken across the Neutral Strip and down into Texas where they were rescued a few days later in the Palo Duro canyon by friends from Woodsdale.

In the fall of 1887 the sheriff's election took place, and John M. Cross, the people's candidate, defeated Dalton, the citizen's candidate, by a majority of three. Cross lived near Woodsdale and Dalton lived at Hugoton. The election was contested, but the courts decided in Cross' favor. He was a very peaceable man, and had never been mixed up in the feuds existing between Hugoton and Woodsdale. In the convention that nominated Cross, Sam Robinson was a candidate for the place. He was engaged in the hotel business at Woodsdale and was one of the most ardent champions of that place. After he failed to get the nomination he moved to Hugoton where he was soon afterwards made city marshal.

[85]

In June, 1888, the question of voting $100,000 in bonds to the Rock Island Railway company, in consideration of the company building two lines of road through the county, was presented to the people of Stevens county. The people of Hugoton bitterly opposed the proposition, but it carried. This intensified the feeling between the two places. A few days before the election, while the question was being discussed at Voorhees, another town, a row broke out and Sam Robinson commanded the peace. Ed Short, deputy sheriff of the county, was present and Robinson struck him. A warrant for Robinson's arrest was issued by the justice of the peace at Woodsdale.

Short went to Hugoton to arrest Robinson and a shooting scrape took place between them and Short was forced to leave without his man. The friends from both towns flew to arms and a conflict was imminent, but the governor sent troops to Stevens county and prevented it. Short retained possession of the writ and on Saturday, July 21, 1888, he received information that Sam Robinson, O. J. Cook, C. E. Cook and A. M. Donald were down in the Strip fishing. Next day, in company with three men, Short started out to capture Robinson.

He learned that Robinson and party were at Patterson's ranch, on Goff Creek, which they surrounded as well as they could. A note was sent to Robinson, demanding his surrender. He declined and, mounting a race horse, dashed away. Short and his men gave chase. A messenger was sent to Woodsdale for Sheriff Cross to come with more men. The messenger arrived at Woodsdale at dark on Tuesday, July 24. Cross immediately summoned Rollin Wilcox, R. T. Hubbard, C. W. Eaton and Herbert Tonney to go with him to aid Short. They left Woodsdale about 9 o'clock Tuesday night and about 8 o'clock Wednesday morning they reached Reed's ranch, but neither Short nor Robinson was there.

After searching in the vicinity of Reed's camp all day

and failing to find either Short or Robinson, Cross and his men started back to Woodsdale. About 9 o'clock, the night of July 25, they reached the head of Wild Horse lake, where a party of four men were camped cutting hay, about eight miles from the Kansas line. As the sheriff and his men had ridden almost continuously for twenty-four hours they concluded to rest awhile before proceeding to Voorhees, where they expected to get food and sleep. They unsaddled their horses and staked them out. Two of the men, Eaton and Wilcox, got in a wagon and Cross, Hubbard and Tonney lay down on some hay.

The moon was just rising. About an hour after they had lain down they were suddenly surrounded by a body of men, when Cross, Hubbard, Wilcox and Eaton were killed and Tonney was wounded and left for dead.

After the massacre the hay men wanted to know what they must do, as they were afraid that if the Woodsdale people should come there and find the dead bodies that they, too, would be killed. They were directed by the killers to hitch up their horses and were escorted across the Kansas line to their homes, about twelve miles away.

As soon as the attacking party had gone away Tonney arose and got his horse, but was too weak and sick to mount. He walked and led his horse until morning, frequently stopping to lie down from pain and exhaustion. When daylight came he found some water and after drinking and washing he got on the horse and rode to Voorhees.

When they reached home one of the haymakers went to Voorhees and told the people what had been done. A courier hastened to Woodsdale with the news and a party started at once in a wagon after the bodies. While on their way they were met by a party from Hugoton who forced them to go on to that place. They were sent from there to Voorhees. On this account it was nearly thirty-six hours before the bodies of Cross, Hubbard, Eaton and Wilcox were removed from the place where they were slain. This,

[87]

too, in the broiling heat of a July sun. Returning with the bodies, they were met and made to drive through Hugoton. When Hugoton people looked in the wagon and saw four bodies instead of five, they knew there was trouble for them.

Attorney General Bradford of Kansas went to Stevens county and made a thorough investigation of the matter and in his report to Governor Martin he characterized it as a cruel murder for which there was no excuse or justification. As the Kansas State court had no jurisdiction to try the case, at General Bradford's suggestion Robinson and his associates were indicted by the United States grand jury at Leavenworth in October, 1888, but the case was dismissed because the Kansas Federal court had no jurisdiction.

By the act of congress of March 3, 1889, establishing a court at Paris, Texas, No Man's Land was placed in the eastern district of Texas. In October, 1889, Robinson and twenty-nine others were indicted there. When arrested they raised the question of jurisdiction before Judge Foster at Leavenworth. He decided in favor of the Paris court. The defendants appealed to the circuit court, but Judge Brewer sustained Judge Foster and the defendents were taken to Paris and tried for their lives.

The six found guilty by the jury were C. E. Cook, his twin brother O. J. Cook, J. B. Chamberlain, Cyrus Frease, J. Lawrence and John F. Jackson, the latter a son-in-law of Chamberlain. Not guilty by the verdict were William O'Conner, A. M. Donald, Smith Grubbs, J. W. Calvert and John A. Rutter, and a mistrial as to Ed Bowden. "No prosecution" had been recommended in the case of nine others indicted, and this was approved by the court, and another nine had not been arrested. Among them was Sam Robinson who had gotten into trouble in Colorado after the killing and was in the Colorado penitentiary.

On June 17 Ed Bowden, one of the defendants, became

[88]

ill and was sent to a hospital on recommendation of a physician, and the case was suspended until June 25. Bowden was then in court but became ill again about noon and agreement was made to enter a mistrial as to him.

When the trial began, 57 of the 60 veniremen summoned were present and of these the Government and the prosecution each challenged three peremptorily, two jurors were accepted, the others disqualified. Next day another venire of 60 was in court and the jury was selected. The defense offered the usual objections, as to the jurisdiction of the court, the method of selecting and summoning the veniremen, what lawyers call motions to "save the point" meaning that they might be upheld in an appeal, and also as usual these were overruled. Nearly three hundred witnesses were then sworn and put under the rule.

The Government was represented by District Attorney J. E. McComb and his assistant, R. E. Hannay, and Sam Wood and an attorney named Williams had been privately employed to assist the prosecution. The defendants had Jake Hodges of Paris, former Attorney General Bradford of Kansas, and two other attorneys, Gordon and Pancoast, all of whom addressed the jury, when the testimony closed.

Herbert Tonney, the young man who was wounded and left for dead, told the story. He said he and his companions were awakened and ordered to put up their hands, which they did, being unarmed. Sheriff Cross, C. W. Eaton, Bob Hubbard and R. T. Wilcox were shot and killed. Tonney was wounded in the left shoulder and fell to the ground. He said they had been searched for arms but had none as they had left their Winchesters strapped to the saddles. "Robinson said, 'Sheriff Cross, you are my first man,' and killed him with a Winchester bullet. He then turned and said, 'Hubbard, I want you too,' and shot him. J. B. Chamberlain, chairman of the board of Stevens County commissioners, leveled his Winchester at me and fired. As he did so I made a slight movement to my right and the

[89]

shot struck my shoulder and knocked me down. When I realized the situation I feigned death.

"Eaton and Wilcox had been asleep in the wagon and hearing the shots got out and were shot, Eaton running several yards before he was killed. Then the four were shot again to make sure they were dead. Wilcox was groaning and they shot him again to 'put him out of his misery.' Someone pulled me by one foot, and lighted a match to look at me to see if he knew me. He did not, and said I should be shot again but Chamberlain said no use, as he had made a center shot. Then they left and presently I got up, looked at the four dead men, caught a horse but was too faint to get on him. I walked till daylight, found a buffalo wallow with some water in it, drank and bathed my wound, managed to ride a little but had to stop and lie down several times. When near Voorhees I met a party coming to see about us and they took care of me."

Tonney was under fire by the defense four hours after his direct testimony, but was not shaken. Apparently the defense was trying to lay a predicate to impeach him. The defense started to offer some testimony bearing on some ancient history of the county seat war, but Judge Bryant stopped it, saying dryly that he wanted no more Kansas history than was necessary.

One of the haymakers, who had not been available earlier, testified as to the shooting, and that Cross' party fired no shots. He identified six of the men on trial as being present at the killing. Four of them, he said, were not there and they had not been named by Tonney in his testimony.

Two physicians testified they had examined the wounds in the bodies and that all four had two or more wounds, one at least of which showed it was made while each man was lying down. Tonney's wound, they testified, must have been made while his arm was raised. While defense witnesses were testifying the attorneys tried to offer testi-

[90]

mony that Sheriff Cross had made threats against Sam Robinson, but Judge Bryant refused to admit it because Sam Robinson was not on trial. (He was in the Colorado penitentiary for post office robbery.) The trial was dragging along and Judge Bryant said that thereafter the Court would remain in session nine hours daily, from 8 to 12 and from 2 to 7 o'clock.

Where the Government made its error was in putting J. B. Bradford on the stand in order to impeach certain defense witnesses. Bradford was attorney general of Kansas when the killing occurred, went to Stevens county and reported to the Kansas governor the killing was cold-blooded murder. By the time the trial in Paris came on, his term as attorney general had expired and he was employed by some of the defendants as counsel. On the stand he denied some of the statements in his report, saying he was misinformed at the time. The admission of this report, or parts of it, in the trial in Paris, was the basis for reversal by the Supreme Court. One of the attorneys for the prosecution, in his address to the jury, referred to the Bradford report and to his testimony on the stand, and said, "There, gentlemen of the jury, you have it—Bradford versus Bradford."

The jury had come into court Monday, after considering the case over Sunday, and told Judge Bryant they thought they could agree as to some of the defendants, but not on others. The foreman handed the judge a paper, apparently what they would return as a verdict, and after reading it Judge Bryant handed it back and told them to consider further. Defense counsel excepted to this and Judge Bryant asked if they demanded the verdict shown him. To this they made no response. The judge told the jury to retire until they agreed or until the defendants would accept the verdict shown him. They did retire and returned their verdict next morning.

The Deputy U.S. Marshals

WHEN THE Federal Court, Eastern District of Texas, Paris Division, held its first sitting, April 29, 1889, Dick Reagan, a brother of Senator John H. Reagan was Marshal. As his term was expiring, and Ben Harrison had become President, Reagan was not reappointed, and a Republican, J. J. Dickerson, of Fort Bend County, was named. The Eastern District extended from Galveston to the Red River, and the Paris Division had been given jurisdiction over the Choctaw and Chickasaw Indian Nations and over the western end of what is now Oklahoma and was then Oklahoma Territory.

It was necessary for Marshal Dickerson to have many deputies, and at times he had as many as seventy-five or eighty, busy serving warrants and making arrests in the area north of Red River, where every crime and misdemeanor known to man was being committed, from introducing whisky into the forbidden area to cold-blooded, deliberate murder. The Indian tribal courts retained jurisdiction over their own people, but where a non-citizen was implicated, either as an offender or a victim, or if the offense was in Oklahoma Territory, the case was brought to the Paris Court.

These deputies had to be fearless and active men—and they were. Some of them had been deputies for the Fort Smith court presided over by Judge I. N. Parker, others had been peace officers in Texas. Marshal Dickerson himself was not unacquainted with handling criminals, for he had been a county officer in Fort Bend County, in the time of the Jaybird-Woodpecker feud. But that is another story, not belonging to a chronicle of the Red River Valley. If it has not been told it should be and by someone who can get the facts after more than fifty years.

One man whom Dickerson employed was Tom Smith. He had been a deputy sheriff in Fort Bend County, and not

[92]

only knew the smell of powder but the effectual use of it. Smith was born in Williamson County, farmed when a youth, gravitated to Fort Bend County where straight shooters were in demand, and presently was called back to Williamson County to be City Marshal in Taylor. In that town a saloon was headquarters for a tough gang and Smith dropped in to tell the "boys" he was in town, not looking for trouble, and asking them to help him keep the peace, which theretofore had been badly shattered. The saloon keeper ordered Smith to get out of his saloon and told him if he came back it would be "just too bad." Some time later Smith did go back to ask about a complaint that had come to him officially, the saloon keeper reached for a gun, but Smith beat him to the draw and the saloon keeper died with a bullet in his body.

Smith was afterwards a deputy sheriff in Williamson and then in Fort Bend and it was with a record of being an efficient officer that Dickerson brought him to Paris and made him a deputy. After four years service and Dickerson's term had expired, and he was replaced by a Democrat under Cleveland's second administration, Smith went to Wyoming to work for some cattlemen who claimed they were being robbed by rustlers. The cattlemen sent him back to Texas to get some men who knew how to shoot, to be used against the rustlers as the courts seemed unable to stop them. The Wyoming situation was mismanaged. Two rustlers were shot. The people generally seemed to think branding a stray calf did not deserve shooting and they rallied to the support of the rustlers and cornered the cattlemen's gun men. They were saved by a troop of U. S. Regulars from a nearby fort, who took them to Cheyenne where they were released on bond, pending trial. Smith returned to Oklahoma and was a deputy for one of the courts that had been established there. He did not answer the summons to the trial in Cheyenne.

Smith and Dave Booker, a deputy, were on a train in

[93]

the Territory and a Negro desperado was on the same train. Booker was on the platform of the end of the car for Negroes and Tom Smith walked into the car, looking for Booker. He had a warrant for the Negro but did not know him, so was not aware that the wanted man was in the car. The Negro knew Smith, however, and knew he had a warrant for him. He evidently thought Tom was looking for him, so he drew his pistol and fired without warning and Smith fell dead in the aisle. Booker heard the shot and looking through the window at the end of the car saw Tom fall and the Negro standing with his pistol smoking. Without an instant hesitation Booker broke the glass with his pistol and fired three shots into the Negro's breast, the wounds so close together they could have been covered by a silver dollar. Tom Smith was avenged, and promptly. Dave Booker was a fearless and efficient officer. Some time before becoming a deputy marshal he had been on the Paris police force where he had learned how to deal with some bad men.

Smith liked to give newspaper reporters a good story. He told O. H. P. Garrett, a reporter for The Paris News, that he had been overtaken by darkness while hunting for a man for whom he had a warrant. There was a house in a grove and it was empty, but it was one that had been abandoned by an Indian family after one of the family died in it, and Indians would not live in a house where one had died. So he wrapped his blanket about him and with his saddle for a pillow lay down to sleep. Rain began to fall, so he got up and went into the house. He fell asleep and was wakened by a scratching and growling and a sound as if somebody was running around the walls of the house and wanted out. It disturbed his sleep so that he finally got up and opened the door and a panther walked out. Smith said he went back to sleep and slept soundly until morning. The reporter printed the story and left it to readers to draw their own conclusions.

[94]

Deputy Marshal Bill McCall came to Marshal Dickerson's office, but without his man. He had been after Black Tiger, a Creek Indian outlaw, and the marshal and his posse (they usually had two or three men with them when expecting to go after a desperate character) had surrounded Tiger in a lot that was fenced. Tiger got on his horse and put the animal over the fence. He and the officers exchanged shots but the outlaw laid close to the horse's back and escaped across the Canadian River into the Creek Nation. He had been chased by deputy marshals of the Fort Smith and Paris courts for ten years.

One of Marshal Dickerson's most efficient deputies was Jim Chancellor, who told of the Davis gang that robbed trains and did every other sort of meanness known to man. They had a hideout in the Arbuckle Mountains where a house was built against the side of a mountain and a room was cut in the mountain, opening from a room in the house. The officer got information that the gang was in the house and he and a posse went to the place at night. When the outlaws began stirring after day the battle was on. Eight were killed or captured but Bill Davis, the leader, escaped. The officers later returned to the place and made a search, finding saddles, bridles, ammunition and other things the Davis gang might need in their outlawry. A dog with the officers sniffed at a crack in the wall and they found the door to the room cut from the mountain. When they opened the door they found a man chained to the wall and more arms and food that had been stored there. They released the chained man, who had been held by the gang on suspicion that he was an informer.

Chancellor once had a warrant for Bill Poe, a noted whisky runner. He did not know where Poe's home was and called on Jesse Perkins, a preacher, who was well acquainted with that part of the country and its people. Chancellor asked Perkins to show him where Poe lived and the preacher agreed to do this and asked to assist Chancel-

[95]

lor and his posse in making the arrest. Chancellor thought this dangerous for the preacher and told him to stay with the horses a little distance from the house where Poe was thought to be.

It was still dark when the posse reached the place and Chancellor stopped in front of the house, sending the others to surround it. When it was light enough to see, the people in the house had apparently seen some of the officers. Bill Davis jumped out the door, with his Winchester rifle and passing to the left of Chancellor tried to get to his horse. Chancellor called to him to drop his rifle and surrender. Davis turned, saw the officer and turned to shoot at him, but Chancellor saw the move and fired. Davis fell dead.

Poe came to the door and called to Davis, asking if he was hurt, and Chancellor called to him to come out and surrender. Poe stepped back out of sight, his wife came to the door, Poe stood behind her, and took a shot over her shoulder at the officer but missed and he and his wife stepped out of sight. This was repeated and Chancellor, still kneeling in front of the house, was shot at a second time but missed. He then began shooting into the house and Mrs. Poe came to the door and called to him for God's sake to stop shooting. Chancellor told her if Poe did not come out and surrender he would shoot the house down. Poe came out with his hands up and the officer handcuffed him. The other men of the posse came up and took charge of Poe. Going into the house, Chancellor found he had shot through a quilt over twin babies, without injuring them, and had smashed the head of a sewing machine. He took what whisky was found in the house for evidence and with Poe and the posse went to where the horses had been left in charge of the preacher and found Perkins dead. One of the bullets fired at Chancellor had struck the preacher who was staying with the horses. Chancellor said that if he had known Perkins was shot before he handcuffed Poe

[96]

he would have killed the whisky runner instead of arresting him. The affair broke up the notorious Davis clan, and Poe, the whisky runner, was brought to Paris and convicted in the Federal Court and sent to the penitentiary.

Heck Thomas, who served under Dickerson and his successor, J. Shelby Williams, had been an express guard on trains west from Fort Worth and had killed or captured several train robbers. He came to Paris and enlisted with Marshal Dickerson, served as a deputy in Oklahoma after courts were established there, and was a peace officer in Lawton at the time of his death.

One day a wagon train drove up to the door of the jail in Gainesville, Texas, and the sheriff saw two heavily armed men get out, open the endgate of the wagon and lay a dead man on the jail porch. When Sheriff Ware and a deputy who was in the office at the time went outside, there were two dead men on the porch. The larger of the two men who had driven the wagon, and who the deputy sheriff afterwards said "Had eyes like black diamonds, a rather long mustache, looked like something carved in bronze, and was the handsomest picture of a man I ever saw," spoke to Ware and asked if he was the sheriff of Cooke County. Ware replied that he was, and the man said, "I am Heck Thomas, operating on a commission out of the Federal Court in Paris. My partner is Jim Taylor who rides the Choctaw and Chickasaw Nations as a deputy from Paris."

Sheriff Ware expressed pleasure in the introduction and asked who were Thomas' friends, laying on the porch. Thomas said, "They are what is left of Jim and Pink Lee, bad hombres from Indian Territory. We left their partner, Smoky Joe, laying in a pasture in Scivills Bend on Red River. He was excess baggage and we told a ranchman where to find him, knowing he wouldn't run away. What I want a receipt from you for the bodies of Jim and Pink Lee, delivered here at Cooke County jail door. It's like

[97]

this. The Lees have run all over the cow camp of the Roff Brothers in Chickasaw Nation, killed two of the Roff boys and Jim Guy, brother of Governor William Guy of the Chickasaw Nation. Alva Roff, the live brother, offered a reward of $7,000 for delivery of Jim and Pink Lee at your jail door. Here they are and I want a receipt as provided in the reward notice."

Sheriff Ware said he would give the receipt for two dead men but he did not know the Lee boys and could not say it was they. Then Heck asked for a sheet of paper, scribbled a notice of delivery and claim of the reward, and tacked it to the bulletin board, using a six-shooter butt for hammer. By this time some rubber-necks had gathered and a hack driver after looking at the bodies said, "Them's Jim and Pink Lee." Then a bartender for a saloon on the court square said, "Damn if they ain't." A blacksmith, a livery stable boss and several others added their identification, so Sheriff Ware gave Heck the desired receipt. The two officers returned to their wagon and left with the team in a long lope for Indian Territory.

Heck afterwards told the deputy sheriff of how the Lees and Smoky Joe were killed. He said he was an express guard and one day saw the notice of the reward offered by Roff. He was an old-time friend of Jim Taylor, then a deputy marshal in Oklahoma. He took leave of absence from the Express company, rode into Oklahoma, met Taylor and agreed on hunting the Lees. Heck got a commission as a deputy marshal and they decided to wait and catch the Lees south of Red River if possible, because both had married Indian women, had friends in Chickasaw Nation and trying to get them there would mean fighting them on their own ground.

They began trailing the gang, and presently the Lees and Smoky Joe crossed the river and riding up the bluff to level ground cut a wire fence and bedded down for the night in a pasture. Heck and his partner followed and hid

[98]

in the grass near where the outlaws had laid down. When the Lees rose about daylight, Heck called to them to surrender and they replied by shooting, one firing from his hip as he rose. Heck Thomas and Jim Taylor replied and the three outlaws fell. Jim went to a ranch and borrowed a wagon and team, loaded in two bodies and took them to Gainesville. They took the sheriff's receipt to Roff and he paid them the $7,000. Thomas later did excellent service in Oklahoma for courts that were established there.

Sometimes the officers lost their lives. One such case was that of Deputy Marshal Carlton of the Fort Smith Court, who was in Denison, Texas, in November, 1887, on the trail of a Negro whisky peddler, named Hogan, wanted in Fort Smith. The Negro was located at the home of a Negro woman and Carlton went to the house with a posseman who was left to guard the front door while Carlton walked to a side entrance and spoke to a Negro woman about doing some washing. He saw the Negro, Hogan, through a door partly open and drawing his pistol ran into the outer room calling to the Negro to surrender. Hogan fired twice and Carlton fell, but fired several shots while he was down, none of which struck the Negro, who left the house by a rear door and escaped.

The officer was taken to a white family residence and attended by doctors but he died after a few hours. He asked that his wife, living in Searcy, Arkansas, be notified and told that he died happy. The body was sent to Hackett City, Arkansas, for burial. Carlton was about fifty years old and had been a member of First Texas Confederate Infantry in the war. He had been with U. S. Secret Service before taking work as a deputy marshal.

The Negro, Hogan, was arrested a few days later in Fort Worth as he got off a freight train where he had hidden and was taken back to Denison, because of a wreck on the railroad between Fort Worth and Sherman, where he was to be put in jail, pending transfer to Fort Smith. The

[99]

officers started to Sherman with him in a hack and a crowd of angry men tried to pull the Negro from the hack and execute him, but the officers succeeded in holding them off and the Negro was taken to Sherman and put in jail.

Deputies from the Fort Smith Court who arrested men in the western part of the Territory generally brought them to Paris over the Santa Fe and Texas and Pacific Railroads, then went to Fort Smith over the Frisco, in preference to the long overland trip across the Territory. One afternoon in 1888 Deputy Marshal W. H. Carr and two guards came to Paris with four prisoners. They were, said Carr, the hardest citizens he had handled that summer. The lot included:

Isaac Frazier, Negro, charged with horse stealing, out of the penitentiary only two months where he had served a term for a previous horse theft; William Bane, charged with robbery after he stopped a man on the street in Purcell, Oklahoma, the night of July 4, and robbed him of $105 and a six-shooter; another man, not named, was charged with introducing whisky into the Territory; the fourth was T. J. Waitman alias George Thorne, charged with horse stealing and said to be wanted in Grayson county for murder. The fellow claimed he was one of the gang that held up and robbed the Missouri Pacific train near Muskogee not long before, though this may have been talk such as the gangsters sometimes made.

Deputies Bob Hutchings and Bud Trainor, in 1896, shot and killed Jim July alias Jim Starr when he resisted arrest. He was Belle Starr's last "husband" and was called by her name. Jim was an Indian and was out on bond to appear in Fort Smith for an offense when Belle was killed. Jim was so interested in trying to find who killed Belle that he forgot to be in Fort Smith on the date set for his appearance. His bondsmen offered a reward and the two deputies were after it. However the bondsmen had withdrawn the offer when they learned Jim's reason for not showing up. The

[100]

officers did not know of this when they attempted to make the arrest.

Sometimes the deputies had to stand trial. One such case was in the Summer, 1893, when the Fort Smith court tried three Paris deputies—Frank Fore, Bill McCall and Ran Dickerson, the latter a brother of Marshal J. J. Dickerson of the Paris Court, for murder, and jury acquitted them. In January, 1892, the deputies were looking for members of what was known as the Gordon gang, charged with horse stealing, robbery and sundry killings, and had struck their trail. They came to a store kept by Caesar Bruner and stopped to get something to eat. Not expecting to find there anyone they wanted, Bill McCall went to the horse lot to see old man Bruner about supper, and there saw several members of the Gordon gang and began shooting. Wash Bruner, a son of the old man, came into the lot with a gun and the deputies said he fired three shots at them, whereupon they shot and killed him. His gun showed three shots had been fired. The Gordons made their escape in the darkness but were caught later, and five were tried, convicted and given penitentiary sentences. The killing of Wash Bruner was in Fort Smith Court's jurisdiction, so the deputies were tried there.

When deputies came in with prisoners or empty-handed they reported to the Marshal and made out a bill of expenses for travel, subsistence and other items. One of the most remarkable was once made to Marshal J. J. Dickerson by Bob Nester, one of his deputies. Nester was a small bowlegged weazened man, with a face burned by sun and wind and creased like a ripe persimmon. Among the items on his report was one for "Killing and burying Shoofly, $6.00." Shoofly was an Indian outlaw for whom Bob had a warrant, and had to be killed when he resisted arrest. Then, as he had no friends to do the work, Bob had to bury him, so he dug a grave and planted Shoofly, charging what he thought to be fair.

[*101*]

JUDGE LYNCH'S COURT

"It is unlawful to overcome crime by crime."—Seneca.

"Crime is not punished as an offense against God, but as prejudicial to society."
—Froude

THERE HAVE BEEN lynchings in the Valley, just as in many other areas, but most of them, especially in the early days, were done openly and sometimes by sentence of a "citizens court." Others were perpetrated by mobs which concealed their identity. In none of the cases, however, was it ever claimed the wrong man or men were executed.

Perhaps the earliest, at least of record, was told of by George W. Wright in his written reminiscences of early Texas. Living in the Pecan Point area on Red River were Captain Charles Burkham and Levi Davis, prominent men. In 1837 some Negroes belonging to them ran away. The owners traced them to the Sabine River, expecting to hear something of them from the Cherokee Indians living thereabouts. They did not find the Negroes and started back home, stopping at the house of a man named Page to get food and to feed their mules which they were riding.

When the two failed to return home friends went in search and did not find them. Some time later a neighbor of Burkham riding through that section met a man riding Burkham's mule which he recognized, having seen Burkham riding it many times. A large party of men went down and took old man Page, his son, Page's son-in-law named Moore and a Mexican who lived with Page. From the Mexican they got a confession and young Page then told the whole matter and showed them where Davis and Burkham had been killed. Some personal belongings of the men were also found, so they took Page to Clarksville and laid the matter before a gathering of the citizens there. Page was sentenced and hanged on the limb of a blackjack tree, which so long as it stood was known as Page's Limb.

Incidentally, Mr. Wright told of a United States deputy marshal coming to Clarksville in 1839, from Arkansas, while that state still claimed what Texas called Red River County was a part of Miller County, Arkansas. The officer

[105]

had a judgment from the Arkansas Federal Court against a Red River County man, and levied on the man's Negro slaves. The sheriff of Red River County arrested the marshal and held him to appear at the next District Court in Clarksville. Mr. Wright said the marshal was really a clever fellow but he thought his power supreme though he had been advised by friends in Arkansas before he left not to try to serve the writ, and, said Mr. Wright, "I guess he would have been willing to give the best hen in his yard to be back home when he had to knock under to the Texas officer. Page's Limb was pointed out to him and its use explained and he got friends in Clarksville to go bail for him and went back to Arkansas."

In August, 1844, a band of friendly Shawnee Indians was camped on a creek in what became Hunt County. The camp was visited by four white men who killed several Indians and took their horses and the furs they had trapped. The settlers knew other Shawnees who were absent from their camp at the time would know the killings had been done by white men, and would probably take revenge on helpless settlers. Citizens from the surrounding area were called and an Indian youth who had escaped the killing told them he knew one of the men named Jones. This man was known to be member of a gang that had a bad reputation, and three of them were arrested with some of the stolen horses and skins. Jones had heard of what was going on and had decamped, but was followed and brought back. A jury of twelve men was formed, trial was held, verdict of guilty was returned and the four were hanged from a limb of a big tree and buried near the place. Their names besides Jones were said to be Mitchell, Rhea and White. Four other men accused of minor thefts were whipped and ordered to leave the country.

Some years before this, in the 'thirties, there was a double hanging in the vicinity of Clarksville, the story coming from a diary kept by a man at that time and handed

[*106*]

down to his family descendants. He said a man named Brooks was killed by a party of men traveling through the country, and gave their names as Fortner, Craig, Hill and Robinson. Clues led to arrest of Fortner and he and his son confessed Brooks had been killed for his money and that a Negro man had also been killed. Fortner told where the other members of the party had gone. Craig was traced to Missouri, caught and brought back, and he and Fortner were hanged on Page's Limb. Hill was caught and whipped, as he was believed to have had no part in the actual killing, and Robinson was never found.

In April, 1863, Mrs. Margaret McCuistion was found dead from deep cuts in her throat, near her home southeast several miles from Paris. She was the wife of M. H. McCuistion, who was Lamar County tax collector several years until he resigned to enter the Confederate Army two years before. She had received a letter from her husband in the Army, and was riding to take it to his aged mother who lived about a mile away. Returning home on the Sunday evening she took a footpath that was a nearer way than the road and as she reached the crossing of a little creek a young Negro man named Rube, who belonged to her husband, sprang from a clump of bushes and pulled her off her horse. She was young and strong and resisted, but he cut her throat and left her body on the bank of the creek, where it was found by relatives searching for her when she did not return home.

Several incidents led the people to believe the Negro was guilty and he was taken into custody and finally confessed, telling of how he had killed the woman. When the news began to spread people gathered from several miles around. There was no thought of appealing to the court, for the crime was one calling for swift punishment. At least seventy-five men, all old because the young men were in the Army, and a number of women and children were in the crowd. It was determined the Negro must die and the

[107]

method was left to vote of all present. The vote was 46 for burning at the stake and 36 advocated hanging, so he was fastened to a post, wood piled about him, and burned until nothing was left but ashes and some charred bones. It could not be called mob action, for it was open and done in daylight.

Jernigan Thicket was a hideout for outlaws for years. It was in the northeast corner of Hunt County and extended into Fannin County and Delta County, which was then a part of Lamar County. It was about ten miles square, somewhat longer than wide, a growth of haw, locust, elm, bois d'arc, cane, and briars, so thickly undergrown that one had to cut his way through it with a cane knife or an axe. There were few trails through which one could ride, and the place was a refuge for lawbreakers of many sorts.

A peddler traveling through the country near the Thicket disappeared. A woman of not too savory reputation lived near and had some articles known to have been offered for sale by the peddler, which she claimed to have bought from him. She and her two sons were arrested and she was tried and sentenced to life imprisonment. All the jurors except one wanted to hang her. That one said that only one woman had been hung in the United States, so far as he knew—Mrs. Surratt who was charged with complicity in a plot to kill President Lincoln and who was hanged—and he did not want Texas to hang a woman. When the case went to the Supreme Court, however, it was reversed and dismissed, as there was no corpus delicti —the peddler's body, if indeed he had been killed, was never found.

During the war between the sections the Thicket was a hiding place for bushwhackers and Union sympathizers who perpetrated many outrages on the families of the men in the Confederate Army. When those men came back— those who could come—they rounded up a gang of guerillas and there was a hanging near Sulphur Springs after

[108]

semblance of a trial in the form of a court martial. Then when Federal soldiers came to take charge of Texas some of the more prominent in the court martial found it advisable to leave the country until things quieted and the soldiers went away.

Something similar to that happened in Lamar County. When the war ended and the men came home, some with one leg or arm, some with a bullet yet in their body or with the scars of a saber cut or bayonet thrust, and all "broke" financially, it is no wonder that passion ran high and resentment died slowly. Especially was this feeling strong against men who had refused to support the South.

One afternoon a group of men were riding home from Paris, traveling the old National Road of the Republic toward the northeast. They had been drinking some and, as is yet the case under such conditions, they got into an argument based on the war and its effects. There were four men in the party and one, Joseph Subber, who was a northern sympathizer, went further in his argument than the others liked, so they took a lariat from one of the saddles, carried Subber into the woods beside the road, threw one end of the lariat over a limb, put a noose around Subber's neck, hoisted him up and rode away. When his friends found him he was quite dead. Without waiting for the Union soldiers to come, for there was enough law left to not condone such an act, investigation was made and the three men left the neighborhood, one going to Georgia where he lived the remainder of his life, the others staying away several years until they decided the affair had been forgotten. The general opinion was that the crime was not due so much to the partisanship as to the liquor they had drunk.

While the war between the sections was in progress a number of Union sympathizers formed what was called a Clan. They were residents of Grayson, and counties west and south, and were said to number near two thousand.

They had passwords, grips and an oath, were in touch with the Kansas Jayhawkers and expected assistance from Kansas when the uprising they planned should begin. The Confederate Government had ammunition stored in Sherman and Gainesville which the Clan expected to seize and compel the Southerners to come into the Union. In case of failure in the latter they were to blow up the ammunition and attempt to join the Yankee Army somewhere in Kansas or Missouri.

There was a leak and the authorities sent Confederate soldiers to Gainesville secretly and arrested every suspected man they could find and took them to Gainesville. When the Southern friends learned what was intended, feeling ran high and they were for killing the prisoners offhand. It was finally agreed that a jury of twelve should be selected and hear each of the 150 under arrest. The jury was beset with demands for the death of all for fear that if any were spared they might later find ways to kill the jurymen.

Among the jurors were three preachers, the Reverend Thomas Barrett, of the Christian Church and J. N. Hamill and J. R. Bellamy of the East Texas Methodist Conference. Verdict, said Mr. Barrett in his memoirs, was to be by majority vote and the first seven heard were convicted, so he thought it was wrong and started to leave, but stayed when it was decided that two-thirds would be required for conviction. While the jury was sitting information came that Colonel William C. Young had been killed while on a hunt in the river brakes, and this so infuriated the people, said Mr. Barrett, that they prepared to kill all the prisoners that night. They did take fourteen of them and hang them. In order to save money they believed innocent the jury consented to the people taking others and forty in all were hung and two shot when attempting to escape.

This broke up the Clan, said Mr. Barrett, and as members of the jury were threatened by both factions he moved to Mount Vernon, then to Bell County. During Governor Hamilton's administration a grand jury found bills against the jurors, so he went to Mississippi and then to Tennessee and stayed about a year, then returned to Cooke County, stood trial under civil court and was acquitted.

Colonel W. C. Young was a Tennesseean who came to Clarksville, Texas, in 1837 and practiced law. He was twice elected sheriff, then district attorney and with Colonel James Bourland made some reputation as an Indian fighter. He moved to Grayson County in 1851 and served as city marshal at Shawneetown, then entered Confederate service, raised the Eleventh Texas Regiment and took it into active service. His health failed and he returned to Gainesville and was killed, as already told, by some of the Clan.

A son of Colonel Young was said to have traced the murderer of his father, captured him and took him to the place where his father had been murdered and there some of Colonel Young's Negroes hung him.

In 1938 appeared a story of some bones being unearthed in Red River County and beads and other trinkets led to the belief they were the remains of Indians. Cortez and Coronado were talked of but Matthew Watson, living then in Valliant, Oklahoma, told a story indicating they were of much more recent date. He said that his grandfather, George Bagby, returning from the war between the sections, was killed by some western Indians. The Indians were caught by Union soldiers and were being taken to Nashville, Arkansas, for trial. The party had to pass through Clarksville, the home of the Bagbys. The story leaked out about what the Indians had done and a body of men followed the soldiers and came up with them as they were camped on a small postoak prairie, and demanded the prisoners. As the officer was taking them to Nashville to go through formality of a trial, and knew he would have the job of shooting them after conviction, he

[*111*]

turned the job over to the Clarksville people who hung the Indians to the limb of a tree in the grove on the little prairie. They were buried 12 or 13 miles east of Clarksville, down the Mill Creek road, near a place called Pinchem. Indians in those days, said Mr. Watson, wore beads and anything ornamental, and "I am willing to bet the bones recently found are those of the Indians who killed one of my grandfathers."

Horse thieves were lynched also, though their passing was not generally so named. In 1874 the Denison News said, "Two horse thieves passed through the city this morning closely followed by several men from Montague County. One of the latter was in Denison later in the evening and said the thieves were overtaken about four miles from Denison and were 'disposed of.' Whether that expression meant that they took gymnastic exercises at the end of a rope we leave our readers to determine." Three weeks later the Denison News said, "A man named Welch was shot by Tom Richards of Sherman near Murman Grove. Welch had stolen two mules from a man living between Sherman and Pilot Point and Richards was attempting to arrest him. When Richards came on Welch the latter attempted to raise a shotgun to his shoulder, when Richards fired, killing Welch. The body was brought to Sherman that night. Welch had stolen the mules from a man named Bean and a horse from a widow living near Pilot Point and the animals were in his possession when he was shot and killed."

In 1872 two horses and a mule were stolen from people living near Deport in Lamar County. Searchers got on the trail and followed it to Little River County, Arkansas, where the sheriff told them the man they described as being about Deport before the horses were stolen was named Coke, who had been in jail several times but managed to escape conviction. The sheriff went with them to Coke's house and arrested him and he was started back to Texas,

[*112*]

the sheriff advising the Texans to ride as fast and as far as possible lest Coke's friends come to his rescue.

When Coke found he was being taken back to Texas rather than the familiar Arkansas jail, he yelled defiance to his captors while riding through the woods next day, and rode off. One of the men headed him and as he did not stop when called on the Texan fired and shot Coke off his horse. He asked to be taken to the sheriff of Bowie County, to whom he would confess, but he died before the sheriff arrived and his body was taken to Boston, Bowie County seat, and delivered to the authorities.

About two years later a man stopped at Lewis Schumann's home near Deport and asked for lodging for the night. He and Schumann sat on the porch after supper and John Grant passed, going to a revival meeting and riding a colt of the mare that Coke had stolen and which had been recovered. Presently Schumann and his self-invited guest went to the meeting and just after they arrived Schumann missed the fellow and found him standing by Grant's colt which was tied on the edge of the ground where the meeting was held. Seeing he was observed the fellow sat on a stump and when service was over both he and the colt were gone.

A brother of Grant, and a friend, learned a man and a colt had crossed Sulphur River. They followed and caught him at Sulphur Springs, brought him back and he was identified by several men who had seen him at the revival meeting. He was under guard at Grant's home and an enraged body of men took him from the guard. Next morning he was found hanging from a limb of an oak tree that stretched over a road about the line of Lamar and Red River Counties.

The man had refused to tell his name or from where he came. There came no one to claim the body and it hung there several days. Then someone dug a hole, cut down the body and put it in the hole and filled it. Some time later

[*113*]

travelers on the road found the hole open and the body was gone, with nothing there except the boots the man had worn. No more horse thefts were reported in that section for many years.

One Saturday in September, 1882, I went with a friend who was employed in Paris to spend Sunday with his parents in Clarksville. There was considerable excitement about a Negro, Wade Bostic, who had been brought to Clarksville from the country and was charged with criminal assault on a white girl seven years old. Bostic was put in jail. There had been no definite proof of his crime at that time, but he was held for investigation by a grand jury.

Just one month later, another Saturday, we went to Clarksville to spend Sunday. The Negro had been indicted and was in jail awaiting trial. Not long after we boys went to bed we heard a salvo of gunshots and my friend said, "I guess they got the Negro." The next morning we went to a place not far from the jail and saw the body of the Negro, his shirt torn off and his body so full of buckshot holes it looked like a sieve. We learned that the Negro's brother had been sitting on the porch in front of the jail at night, with a shotgun which could be carried legally, but this night he had decided to go to a revival meeting at a Negro church, thinking no attack on the jail would be made so early. However a body of men appeared at the jail and when the jailer asked before opening the door who was there, he was told it was the constable with a man to be put in jail. He opened the door, faced the muzzles of several shotguns and his keys were taken from him. The Negro was taken out and the men started out of town but the prisoner made so much noise that his captors stood him against a fence and shot him. It was fortunate for the brother that he was not at the jail else he also would have been killed. The identity of the lynchers was never disclosed nor was there any great effort made to learn who they were.

[*114*]

EXECUTION OF WILLIAM GOINGS
The Last under Choctaw Law

William Goings, Choctaw Indian, convicted of murder, was shot by the Indian sheriff, July 13, 1899, on Alikchi court ground. Twice postponed, when the execution was carried out, a versifier on the *McAlester Capital* began a jingle, "Has William Goings gone?"

Replying to this, R. J. Long, who sometimes perpetrated rhymes for *The Paris News*, issued a reply, the first verse saying:

> *"Yes, William Goings' gone, dear friend,*
> *He's gone beyond recall.*
> *The Choctaw sheriff honored him*
> *With a big Winchester ball."*

[This is the story I wrote less than 24 hours after I had witnessed the execution of a Choctaw Indian, the last under the tribal laws. I was one of two white men within the lines where others were required to stop, at the court ground. The story is exact in every detail and not from memory years afterwards].

A SHARP REPORT, an echo that sprang from hill to hill in the Sulphur Springs (Alikchi) valley, then silence for an instant—and William Goings, Choctaw Indian, alleged slayer of seven of his relatives, lay on his back, a Winchester bullet letting out his life blood. He had paid the penalty of an outraged law, as administered by the courts of the Choctaw Nation. His death was the final scene in one of the unique cases on the records of Choctaw tribunals of justice.

July 13, 1899, Alikchi court ground was in the hills that begin near Little River and run north to the Kiamichi Mountains. The court house, a frame building much like the typical country school house, stands halfway up one of the hills, at the base of which the sulphur springs burst from the earth. In its rear is the jail, built of heavy squared logs and lined with iron, in which the last days of the condemned man were spent. From this jail he was led to his execution. Once before he had been brought out in obedience to a writ from a Federal Court which was asked to stop execution of the sentence of the Choctaw Court, but which decided it had no authority to do so. Once before, Goings had left the jail, an escaping prisoner, in company with his cousin who was indicted jointly with him, only to be captured after a brief period of liberty and brought back, chains put around his neck and limbs, making escape again impossible.

William Goings was convicted of the murder of a relative, Samson Goings, a Choctaw Indian, in 1896. The homicide was committed in Eagle County, northeast of

[*117*]

Alikchi, and whisky was the cause. Goings and his cousin, a young man named Crosby, had been across the line into Arkansas and got whisky. Returning home they stopped in the road near Samson Goings' home and made noises usually made by drunken persons, with both mouth and pistols. Samson, who recognized the voices and the cause of the noise, went out to partake of the liquor. During the revelry Samson was killed.

The trial of a Choctaw Indian by his native court was not so productive of details of evidence as that which characterizes our tribunals. All that was recorded was that Samson was found dead in the road, the two young men did not deny the killing and they were tried and found guilty. It was said that at different times previously Goings had killed six people, all related to him, one of them a woman. The haze surrounding the words and actions of the fullblood Indian, especially in matters connected with their government, prevented finding many details of the young man's life.

Gathered from various sources it was learned that Goings, at the time of his execution, was about thirty years old; that he married several years before and that his wife was afraid of him, as indeed were most of his family, including his parents. This fear of possibly suffering the fate of the seven gone before led them to show apathy in this young man's case.

It was said openly at the court ground before the execution that they really wanted him executed. Be that as it may, certain it was that no relatives attended him in his last hours, and if any were present at the execution they made no sign that the principal actor in the drama was more than a chance acquaintance.

After the killing of Samson the two young men, Goings and Crosby, were tried at Alikchi, convicted and sentenced to be shot. Their lawyer appealed the case to the Choctaw Supreme Court, sitting at Tushka Humma. After review-

[118]

ing the proceedings the three judges concurred in the verdict of the District Court. The date for the execution drew near and the prisoners escaped. There was a story that one of the Supreme Judges was sorry for the youths, and sent notice to them before the Court's decision was made public, and advised them to get away. They did get out, whether so advised or not. They had been in jail during the bitter cold weather of February, 1899, and before Crosby was captured he died at the home of relatives where he had hidden. His death was from pneumonia, attributed to a cold he contracted while he and William were in jail.

William Goings, bold and defiant, roamed the country almost at will. He had been a member of an Indian ball team that made a trip through the North. It was claimed by some, without any sort of proof, that he had been released by the authorities to play a brief season, at the end of which he would return to the place of execution of his own free will and be shot. That was the custom among the Indians of earlier years, but William had abandoned the customs of his forefathers. He loved life and liberty and was recaptured while visiting some of his people in Eagle County, near the scene of the homicide, put back in jail and chained to the floor. The new date for execution was set for the last day of April.

A few days before that day a writ of habeas corpus was issued by Judge Clayton of the Federal Court in Indian Territory, and Goings was taken before him. The deputy marshal who served the writ arrived at Alikchi the day before that set for the execution, and served the writ on the Choctaw sheriff. Report had it that the officer arrived as Goings was being led out to be shot, that he had surmounted many difficulties in his wild ride to reach Alikchi in time, and that Goings was snatched, as it were, from the jaws of death. This was a pretty story but lacked truth. The deputy marshal passed through Paris on a train and

[*119*]

went on his mission with no more hurry nor incident than if the prisoner had been a whisky peddler.

Goings was taken before Judge Clayton in Atoka, and after reviewing the case Judge Clayton ruled he had been legally tried and convicted and that United States had no authority to interfere. The law known as the Curtis Bill, which took from the Indian courts the power to try capital cases, went into effect June 28, 1898, but cases on the Indian dockets before that date were not affected by it. This seemed to settle the question and after the prisoner was returned to Alikichi, Judge Absalom James came from his home 14 miles away and set July 13 for the execution.

It was rumored all over the east end of the Choctaw Nation that Goings would not be shot; that Judge John R. Thomas of the Territory Federal Court had been appealed to and would grant a new writ of habeas corpus. A deputy marshal at Antlers wired Judge Thomas at Muskogee and got no reply. The Judge was not there. Several other points were tried and it was learned that Judge Thomas would be in Tulsa the afternoon of July 12. The other Federal Judges were out of the Territory at the moment, and Judge Thomas was the only hope of those who were trying to prevent the execution.

At 5 o'clock the morning of July 13 three men rode into Alikchi at a gallop, their horses flecked with foam, the men dirty and tired from an all-night ride from Antlers. Everybody in Alikchi knew in a few minutes that they brought a writ. One of the men was a deputy marshal, the others friends of Goings. They rode to where Sheriff Thomas Watson and some guards sat in front of the jail, and the deputy marshal handed the sheriff a document that read:

"Tulsa, I. T., July 12, 1899. To Thomas Watson, sheriff, Antlers, I. T. You are hereby commanded to have the body of William Goings, detained in your custody as it is said, together with the day and cause of his being taken, before me in the court house in South McAlester, on the 22d day of July, at 10 o'clock in the forenoon, and then and there state in writing the cause of his imprisonment and producing your answer. So doing, and not to fail under heavy penalties of the law against those who disobey this writ, and to submit to and receive all those things which then and there adjudged in this behalf. Given under my hand this 12th day of July, 1899. John R. Thomas, Judge."

The "writ" was a telegraph blank, and pasted to it was a certificate, purporting to be signed by the telegraph operator in Antlers, stating that the writ as copied had been received from Tulsa. The deputy marshal told Sheriff Watson that he was "Warned in the name of United States of America not to proceed with the execution."

Sheriff Watson made no reply. He turned to one of his deputies and together they walked to the Woolry Hotel where Abner Clay, the Choctaw district attorney, was boarding. Abner Clay is a bright young man. He fits the position he fills and all the people know him and respect his judgment. After a brief conference with the sheriff, Clay wrote a note to Judge James, telling him the substance of the writ, and a messenger was sent to the Judge's home near Red River, instructed to cover the 28 miles there and back before noon.

Then things stopped. The people of the little town went about their usual occupations, the several hundred visitors wandered about from the spring to the court house or sat in groups about the stores and wondered what would be the outcome. The sun rose higher until just ten minutes before it reached the meridian the messenger came up the road, spurring his horse, and was met by the district attorney. The impassive countenances of the two betrayed no sign of what was Judge James' answer, as they went into the court house, the crowd following to the doors of the building.

Presently the sheriff and district attorney came from the court house and addressed the crowd, the sheriff speaking Choctaw, the attorney speaking English. The substance of their address was that they described a line from one tree to another, about one hundred yards from the west side of the court house, as the point beyond which no one could pass. They added that the officers would confer and later would execute the orders of their superiors. They did not say what the orders were, and no one knew whether there would be obedience to the writ or execution of a man.

Just before 1 o'clock the conference of the officers ended and announcement was made that Goings would be shot at 2 o'clock. It was revealed that Judge James' reply to the district attorney was that if United States had, at the court ground, any evidence to show that under Federal laws there should be a stay of execution it should be stayed —otherwise it should be done. The Choctaw officials were unanimous in deciding that the telegraphed writ was not sufficient evidence of Judge Thomas' authority; that it was addressed to the sheriff when it should have been addressed to the United States marshal; that it bore no seal, and should have been sealed by the deputy United States clerk at Antlers; and that Judge Clayton, when he dismissed the habeas corpus, had settled the case. Therefore, Goings should be shot.

At 2 o'clock the 20 guards headed by Paul Stevens, the light horse captain (the Choctaw constabulary were called light horse), formed double rank, the files facing the crowd of spectators. From a carpenter shop down the hill four Indians brought a coffin, a plain pine box, roughly covered with black calico, enclosed in an outer box. They set it down near the court house door and wiped the sweat from their faces as they stood stolid-faced, showing no sign of interest in what was to come. A bed quilt folded breadthwise was laid on the ground about fifteen feet in

[122]

front of the court house door. A backless bench was set between the door and quilt. An Indian boy brought a hammer and laid it on the coffin lid. The eight nails in the lid had been driven part way in and shone in the sunlight.

The people west of the court house, along the line described by the officials had increased to about 300. In it were a couple of newspaper reporters, half a dozen amateur photographers, one professional picture taker, white people and Indians, men, women and small children—a sensation-seeking assembly. They waited quietly for the end of the drama which had been so long coming.

They had not much longer to wait.

In the court house were the Indian Clerk of the court, two Indian preachers, Methodists, Reverends Madison Jefferson and Willis Tobely, and I—no one else. Outside the door were the four men who had brought the coffin. In the rear of the court house, between it and the jail, were the files of guards, each armed with a drawn pistol or a rifle carried at arms port, ready for action should a demonstration be made.

At a word from the sheriff the two preachers went into the jail to hold a service, which was conducted in Choctaw. From the rear of the court room the clerk and I could hear the voices of the ministers raised in prayer, reading the Bible and singing hymns. The words, unintelligible to me, were understood by the clerk who bowed his head and sighed. I understood nothing except the familiar air of "Nearer My God to Thee," sung with Choctaw words.

Goings professed religion during his last days and the service in the jail was at his request. No one except the preachers was permitted in the jail during the service. Even the sheriff stayed outside, his rifle leaning against the log walls of the jail, near the door, waiting until the preachers finished comforting the soul of the condemned man.

The religious service lasted 20 minutes. The preachers

[*123*]

came in the court house and sat near the judge's table. Through the open door they could see the folded quilt on which a man was to die. The court clerk walked restlessly about, occasionally speaking to me in answer to a question, or to deplore the necessity of the execution.

The prisoner was brought out of the jail.

Sheriff Watson had loosed his earthly bonds and soon would sever those binding his spirit to his body.

Goings' wrists were crossed in front and handcuffed. A guard held each of his elbows.

The sheriff walked to the left of the prisoner, his rifle resting in the hollow of his left arm.

When they reached a point midway down the two columns of files the guards began to move and the procession passed down the hill from between the jail and the court house.

The jail door was left open and swung idly—there was no longer need to close it.

The guards and prisoner walked straight toward the line of spectators until within 10 feet of the front row, turned sharply to the left and passed along the front of the entire line. Another left turn faced them up the hill and the third turn brought them to the front of the court house where they halted. Then 14 guards faced the spectators and four faced toward the top of the hill where about a dozen people had gathered.

Goings was dressed in the everyday garb of Indians of the neighborhood. His white cotton shirt was figured with a small pink floral pattern, his trousers and shoes were plain black, cheap, and showed signs of ordinary wear. A round flat-crowned brown wool hat, the brim slightly turned up was on his head. He wore no belt or coat.

He walked nearly to the end of the quilt nearest the door of the court house.

The look on his face was that of a man who did not understand what it was all about. He made no show of

[*124*]

indifference, and seemed to be guided in his walk by the two guards who held his elbows.

He sat down on the quilt, far enough forward for his head to be on it when he should lie at full length.

He looked upward once, toward the door of the court house, but his head did not turn toward the right or left.

The sheriff had already prepared the man's breast. With fingers that did not quiver he had unbuttoned the prisoner's shirt from the neckband to the waist, rolled back the edges and turned them beneath themselves, leaving a space a few inches wide. From his coat pocket the sheriff took a small folded paper, opened it and rubbed his forefinger in the soot it contained. With this he made a small round spot on the pale copper-colored skin of Going's breast. It was a little to the right of and below the heart. If he intended it to center the heart he missed it.

Leaning down to the prisoner sitting on the quilt, Sheriff Watson, with a handkerchief in his hand, spoke to Goings who answered by closing his eyelids. The handkerchief was bound over his eyes, shutting out the sunlight forever.

Goings then prayed, speaking in his own language, not loudly but distinctly.

The sheriff stepped behind the low bench, knelt on the ground and rested his rifle on the bench, the muzzle about eight feet from the prisoner's breast.

The two guards who held Goings' elbows also knelt, drawing his elbows out until his handcuffed wrists crossed at his waist.

Sheriff Watson sighted along the rifle barrel, perhaps twenty seconds—who could say? To some it seemed minutes, to others but an instant. I believe the delay, if any, was to allow the prayer of the condemned man to be finished.

Then the rifle spoke.

It was 2:24 by the watch of one of the men in the court

[*125*]

house, with which the sheriff had compared his watch just before he walked to the little bench.

Goings' body fell back and stretched at full length on the quilt. A crimson stream flowed from his breast, dyed the edges of his shirt and trickled on the quilt beneath him.

And then began one of those terrible scenes, sometimes a part of executions by other means.

The man was not dead. His groans could be heard by people several yards away.

His breast heaved, his feet were drawn up, his arms twitched, he seemed to try to raise himself to a sitting position, but the two guards restrained him. And all the time, and above all, his awful death groans.

Presently the sheriff, who had gone inside the court house and sat at a window near me, from which I had looked at the execution, told a guard to bring water. A bucket was brought and with a tin dipper water was poured into Goings' throat, strangling him. A physican was called from the crowd of spectators to determine if the wound was mortal.

Goings was not yet dead, but the doctor said he thought the man could not live an hour. The hemorrhage should kill him by that time, if the water in his lungs did not. The sheriff had apparently mistaken the location of Goings' heart and he was dying slowly. Another doctor, who came a little later, declared the man was dead; that he was shot a little below the heart. The doctor's opinion was that strangulation by the water had been immediate cause of death, though the wound had been a contributory cause.

About an hour after the execution the body was put in the coffin and a relative of Goings took it to Eagle County for burial.

I had gone to Alikchi with Joe McKee, a field deputy marshal for the Paris Court, and two office deputies, the three attending only as spectators and not in an official capacity, as Paris then had no jurisdiction across the river, the Curtis Bill having abolished it. McKee had worked in that country while Paris had jurisdiction, and was well known and universally liked because of his straightforwardness and fairness with the people.

When the line beyond which no one was to pass was described, I told Joe that I wanted to get nearer if possible. He was a man of few words, much like the Indians among whom he had worked many years, and he said nothing. After a while he told me to go on up to the court house. I asked, "What shall I say to the sheriff?" He replied, "Say nothing; just go on up there." He had spoken to Sheriff Watson, telling him a friend with him wanted to be nearer the execution, and the sheriff was glad to oblige McKee.

Just after he fired the shot, Sheriff Watson stepped into the court house. I was standing up and he reached out, I took his hand and we shook hands, not a word being spoken. Then he broke his rifle and the ejected shell fell on the floor. Joe McKee picked it up. I begged him to give it to me but he said he wanted to keep it.

Goings was the eleventh man I have seen die at the hands of the law, the others being hanged in Paris at different times by sentences of the Federal and State Courts. It was part of my work as a news reporter.

When Judge Thomas heard that Goings had been executed he was not pleased. He summoned Sheriff Watson before him for contempt of court. When he learned that Judge Clayton had already passed on the case, and that the application which resulted in Judge Thomas issuing his writ was made by persons who knew Judge Clayton had ruled, he discharged the sheriff and was even more displeased at the persons who had misled him, and it was said that he gave them a good lecture.

SOME ROBBERIES
Stage, Express, Bank, Train

"All men love to appropriate to themselves the belongings of others; it is a natural desire; only the manner of doing it differs."—Le Sage

THERE HAVE BEEN stage, express, bank and train robberies in the Valley, and to tell of all would make too big a book and would be tiresome. A few will suffice to show the methods used and the results.

When the Texas and Pacific Railroad stopped at Brookston, ten miles west of Paris, because the money market dried in 1873, passengers were brought to Paris on a stage. Clarence Green, Paris youth, also ran a hack that carried passengers and parcels. October 7, 1874, the hack left Brookston ahead of the stage. When about three miles from Paris it was stopped by three masked men who demanded to know if the man who killed Jim Reed was in the hack. He was not, and the hack driver was made to turn out of the road, put out his lamps, while the three bandits waited for the stage.

When the stage arrived, it was stopped and the passengers ordered out. The four men passengers obeyed but the two women were allowed to stay inside. The men were searched and their money and watches were taken, estimated to be about three hundred dollars in cash. One of the bandits said the women should be searched, and one of his companions said, "Do you take me for a fool? If you want them women searched, get in and do it yourself." Had the robbers known that one of "them women" had a package of $4,000 currency they probably would have forgotten their gallantry and looked for it.

That money was a package being brought from Kansas City by I. M. Smith, cashier of a recently organized bank in Paris. When the stage was stopped he handed it to his wife who with him was returning from a visit to friends in the north, and she dropped it on the stage floor, hiding it with the hem of her skirt. That was the way the money was saved.

[*131*]

February 4, 1878, the agent for Texas Express Company in Paris told officers he had been robbed of a package containing $10,000, while waiting about midnight at the railroad station to put the package on the train. The Texas and Pacific Railroad had been completed from Sherman to Texarkana and the train from the west arrived in Paris soon after midnight.

John Griffin was the agent and his brother, Maurice, drove the express wagon, but was sometimes relieved by his brother John, and this night was one of such times. The agent said he was standing near the depot by his wagon when two men approached and attacked him, knocking him down, taking the package and running away in the darkness. As soon as he could get up he shot at the men with his pistol, but apparently did no execution. He had a black eye, mud on his face, and a slight wound on one hand.

The express company sent detectives to Paris, and presently the two brothers were arrested and went to trial as soon as the legal steps of indictment and arraignment were taken. The jury returned a verdict of guilt imposing sentences of two years in the penitentiary for each of the brothers. The case was appealed and the Supreme Court of Texas reversed and dismissed it because the men were charged with embezzlement and the evidence failed to show that crime, as set out by the statutes.

At the trial it was shown that the money package had been delivered to John Griffin by J. E. Roberts, cashier of Paris Exchange Bank, to be sent to the bank's correspondent in St. Louis. For the prosecution a salesman in a Paris store testified that several days after the robbery one of the brothers had told him, before they were arrested, that the money was hidden under the Cumberland Presbyterian Church, a few blocks from the square. He testified the brother offered to give him part of the money if he would get it and keep it until things settled down, and that he refused. He said he had gotten a policeman to go with him to the church, they crawled under the building and searched, but no money was found, and that when he told the agent next day he had not found the money the agent seemed surprised.

Solution of the affair came some months later. One of the detectives lived in Memphis, Tenn., and after returning home he was taken ill with smallpox, and died. When he became convinced he would die he said that he had followed one of the brothers one night, who walked around the church building and apparently intended to go under it, but noticing that he was being followed, walked away. The detective said he then went under the church, found the money and kept it.

May 23, 1894, the First National Bank of Longview was robbed. Bill Dalton, Jim Bennett and Bill and Jim Knight, rode up to the bank, stopping in an alley. Bennett led the horses to the rear of the building while Bill Knight stopped in front and Dalton and Jim Knight went in. They had rifles under their raincoats and walked up to the window where two bank officers were talking to a customer, showed their rifles and demanded money. The officers gathered up all the money in sight and handed it over and the two robbers started out.

A man in the rear part of the banking room had slipped out a side door and gave the alarm and citizens with guns began gathering. Bennett, who was guarding the horses, opened fire, killing one citizen and wounding another who died later and still another who recovered. Then Bennett was killed by the shots from several guns in the hands of citizens. The two robbers made the two bank officers come out with them, and using the officers as shields got on their horses, made the bankers get on behind them, and rode away. They were followed as soon as horses could be gotten by Longview officers and citizens, but escaped. The bankers were dropped off when a short way out of town.

J. Shelby Williams, United States Marshal for the Paris Court, had deputies looking for the robbers who were said to have crossed Red River north of Paris, but they were not found. In July a man bought a farm wagon in Ardmore, Oklahoma, and paid for it with $20 banknotes. When they were deposited in an Ardmore bank it was noticed they were issued by the Longview bank and had not been signed by the president and cashier of that bank, as was then the law with respect to national bank notes. Later it was learned that the currency had just been received by the Longview bank and the officers had not had time to sign it before the robbers took it.

The Ardmore banker notified the deputy marshals and several of them went to the home of the farmer who had bought the wagon. They did not expect to find Bill Dalton there, but did expect to make the farmer tell them where he might be found. But Dalton was at the house. Seeing the officers he broke from the house and ran, and one of the deputy marshals killed him with a rifle.

The Knight brothers were not at the place. Later that year they were located by officers in the river bottom in Guadalupe County, Texas. They resisted arrest, one was shot and killed, the other was wounded. He was taken to Longview, got a change of venue to Smith County and was tried and convicted in Tyler and given sentence of 20 years in the penitentiary. After serving several years he was pardoned by Governor O. B. Colquitt, and it was said that he was later killed in a difficulty in Tulsa, Oklahoma.

Bill Dalton was the fourth of five brothers who met violent deaths. Frank, the oldest, never an outlaw, was killed while serving as a peace officer. Bob was the leader of the brothers when they turned to robbery, and he and his brother Grattan were killed in a bank robbery in Coffeyville, Kansas, several years before the Longview affair. Emmett Dalton was wounded in Coffeyville, and had ridden far enough to have escaped but rode back when he found his brothers were not with him, was shot off his horse and captured. He was sent to prison for his part in that robbery and when he was released he decided to live straight. He married, settled down and wrote a book, telling of the exploits of the Daltons and pointing out how certain was the end of lawless men. He said, "If youth were not so headlong—if only it would survey the paths ahead."

Trains on the Katy Rail Road were frequently held up and robbed in the thinly settled Indian Territory. One of the latest was in August, 1901, when torpedoes on the track near Caney water tank, north of Denison, signaled the engineer to stop. When the train was stopped there was some shooting, to frighten the crew and passengers, and two robbers came into the coaches, ordered everyone's hands up, and began taking their money and jewelry. A passenger said the train was stopped nearly an hour while the robbers blew open the express car safe, searched the registered mail and robbed the passengers.

When the people in the chair car realized it was a hold-up a hurried attempt to hide money and valuables was begun. Two masked men came in the coach and with drawn pistols gave the order for hands up. Another, with the mail clerk carrying a mail bag, walked down the aisle and ordered everybody to drop their money in the bag. About forty passengers were in the car and all were robbed except five or six women. One woman gave her purse and a piece of her mind at the same time and the robbers returned her money and let the other women alone. They made the rounds a second time and searched under the cushions to see if anything was hidden.

One passenger, with his wife and baby, saved most of his money. He had his pocketbook in his hand and his wife handed him the baby to hold. When the order for hands up was given he laid down the baby and dropped his pocketbook in the cuspidor. He lost the small amount of cash in his pocket and after the robbers had left he retrieved his pocketbook. [135]

SOME EMINENT MEN

"Greatness, after all, in spite of its name, appears to be not so much a certain size as a certain quality in human lives. It may be present in lives whose range is very small." —*Phillips Brooks*

Two RESIDENTS of the Valley became governors of States—Hardin R. Runnels, of Texas, Robert L. Williams, of Oklahoma. Their terms were almost sixty years apart.

Hardin Richard Runnels was a Mississippian, who came with his widowed mother to Texas about 1842, and settled in Bowie County, where they opened a plantation on rich prairie land near Old Boston. His political career included four terms in the Texas Legislature, speaker of the House the last term, after which he was elected lieutenant governor when E. M. Pease was chosen for a second term as governor. At the end of that term he was elected governor and served one term.

Coming from the only Valley county named for an Alamo hero, Runnels had the added distinction of defeating Sam Houston, who had twice been president of the Republic. He was defeated for a second term by Houston, retired to his plantation and did not again seek office. He was chosen a member of the Secession Convention, 1861, and of the 1866 Constitutional Convention.

Governor Runnels never married. He was engaged to a young woman who lived in Clarksville, and the engagement was broken after the date for the marriage was announced. He had built a two-story mansion near the town of Boston, one of the finest houses in Texas at that time. He died on Christmas Day, 1873, and was buried in the village graveyard.

Robert Lee Williams was born in Alabama, December 20, 1868, educated in Southern University, Greensboro, Alabama, with M. A. degree, and began practice of law in Troy, Alabama. In 1896 he came to Atoka, Indian Territory, and six months later moved to Durant, which was his legal residence until his death, April 10, 1948.

In 1899 R. L. Williams was elected City Attorney of Durant, but resigned before the term ended. He was

[139]

elected a member of the 1906 Oklahoma Constitutional Convention, and had a large part in framing the Constitution. Incidentally he had the Convention to name his county Bryan, in honor of the Great Commoner.

At the first election under the Constitution, he was elected Chief Justice of Oklahoma Supreme Court, preferring it to being Governor, for which office he was urged. He was re-elected Chief Justice for a full term, resigning in 1914 to make the campaign for Governor, to which office he had been nominated by the Democratic Party. He was elected over John Fields, Republican, and served four years, which included the period of World War I.

President Wilson, in 1919, appointed Judge Williams to be U. S. District Judge of Eastern District of Oklahoma, which office he retained until 1937. He was appointed to the bench of the Tenth Judicial Circuit in 1937, and retained this office until early in 1939, when he retired, being 70 years of age. He continued to serve when needed, and often held court in Oklahoma, and in Texas, when asked to relieve a judge of those courts.

When he passed away, Judge Williams was president of Oklahoma Historical Society, member of the Methodist Church, member of the American Bar Association, a Thirty-second Degree Mason. He was never married.

During his administration as Governor the Oklahoma State capitol was built, at a cost of a million and a half dollars. He gave the work much personal attention. The Sixth Oklahoma Legislature met in the uncompleted building in 1917, its most important work being the bill granting the ballot to the women of Oklahoma, the bill being later approved by vote of the men voters of the State.

Judge Williams, in 1935, presided in Durant at the trial of Arthur Gooch who, with a companion later killed in resisting arrest, had kidnaped R. N. Baker and H. R. Marks, Paris, Texas, night policemen who were questioning Gooch and his companion. They took the officers, in the

[140]

police patrol car, into Oklahoma, where they were released next day. The trial was under what is known as the Lindbergh Law, enacted by the Congress after the kidnaping of the Lindbergh baby. Following that kidnaping and later that of an Oklahoma oil operator, Senator Thomas P. Gore of Oklahoma had the Congress to amend the law, adding the death penalty, if recommended by a jury, to the original law that had life imprisonment as the maximum penalty. The jury in the Gooch case so recommended and Judge Williams pronounced the sentence. Gooch was hanged under supervision of the United States Marshal, the first execution under the Lindbergh law.

Some native sons of the Valley attained more than local recognition and rendered service of the highest order. Most prominent of these was John Garner, born in Red River County, November 22, 1869. He attended a country school and played baseball, read law in Clarksville and was admitted to the bar. Practicing there briefly, he was advised by a doctor to go to a dryer climate. He went to Uvalde and there found John Clark and Tully Fuller, who were lawyers in Paris some years before going to Southwest Texas. They made John a junior partner, to attend country courts, which meant riding hundreds of miles. He did so well that they made him a full partner.

Presently John Garner was elected county judge of Uvalde County, four years later went to Texas Legislature, and after two terms he moved to Washington as Representative of Fifteenth District. He was reelected fourteen times and then was chosen as Vice President by F. D. Roosevelt in 1932. At the end of two terms in that office he returned to Uvalde—a man who has earned what he has and who is, as he has always been, a Democrat.

J. O. Richardson, Valley born, graduated from Paris High School and from Annapolis and served in the Navy, advancing in rank through the years until he earned and was given the rank of Admiral. He was briefly commander-

[*141*]

in-chief of the United States fleet, but shortly before Pearl Harbor was attacked by the Japanese he was superseded and ordered back to Washington, when he found himself unable to agree with President Roosevelt on handling the steadily increasing tension with Japan. But for this shift in authority in the Pacific there might have been a different story to tell, with Pearl Harbor omitted.

William Johnson McDonald, born in southern Lamar County, oldest son of Dr. Henry G. McDonald, had an early education at McKenzie Institute near Clarksville. He studied law, but became a banker and invested his earnings and profits until at his death he had accumulated more than a million dollars. He never married and never stopped studying. In his later years he attended some Summer sessions at Harvard. He was interested in astronomy and his will, after providing for some of his relatives, left the bulk of his estate to the University of Texas to establish an observatory. The W. J. McDonald observatory was built in the Davis Mountain of Texas and is one of the best equipped plants for the study of astronomy.

Half a dozen Texas counties are named in honor of men who were early-day Valley citizens and rendered service as Indian fighters or lawmakers or did other things that called for recognition. Richard Ellis was president of the Convention that adopted the Declaration of Independence and a Senator in the first four Congresses. Edward H. Tarrant, Indian fighter, who resigned his seat in the Congress because he believed he could better serve his people by protecting them against Indians. Samuel P. Carson, North Carolina Congressman before coming to Texas, filled many responsible positions in the Republic. William C. Young, jurist and soldier, Mexican war veteran, Confederate officer. Robert Potter, North Carolina legislator and Congressman, signer of the Declaration, secretary of Texas navy and Senator of the Republic. Collin McKinney, signer of the Declaration, for whom a county and county seat are named. [*142*]

SOME PREACHERS

*"I venerate the man whose heart is warm,
Whose hands are pure, whose doctrine and whose life,
Coincident, exhibit lucid proof
That he is honest in the sacred cause."*   *—Cowper*

AND SOME PEOPLE

*"A genial hearth, a hospitable board,
And a refined rusticity."*
             —Wordsworth

WHEN SETTLERS came to the Valley their first action, after selecting the place they were to live, was to cut logs and build their homes. Then churches and school houses were built, sometimes one building being used for both purposes. Until these were built, religious services were held in homes. Many of the people were church members, and even those who were not were glad of the opportunity to attend services when a preacher was available.

Soon after Claiborne Wright arrived at Pecan Point a service was held in his house by William Stephenson, a Methodist preacher. Several years later a camp meeting was held not far from Jonesboro, conducted by Stephenson, Green Orr and Rucker Tanner. Later comers into the Valley were J. W. P. McKenzie and James Graham, both Methodist preachers and school teachers. The Reverend William Brackeen, a Baptist minister, was another early arrival, and many more held services at times as they traveled through the Valley.

The Reverend Mr. McKenzie was probably the best known of these men. He was sent as a missionary to the Choctaw Indians in the Territory in 1836. Then he was transferred to mission work in Texas, his field being from Red River to Sulphur River and from a part of Arkansas on the east to Preston Bend (now in Grayson County) on the west. In early years he held services in homes, there being few church buildings except in county seat towns. His health becoming impaired he settled four miles west of Clarksville's public square, where he built a home and a school. He called the place Itinerant Retreat, and it continued until about 1882. So greatly had the school grown in attendance and importance that in 1854, when the school had been operating more than ten years, the Texas Legislature granted it a charter, under the name of McKenzie Institute. The charter named the founder and

[*145*]

eight prominent men as trustees, and the faculty was authorized to confer degrees. In that school some of the most prominent men of Texas were educated.

McKenzie was fearless and fought the devil any and every place and at any time. While he was a missionary in the Indian Territory he preached against gamblers. The group of card sharpers that had received his condemnation delegated one of their number to whip the preacher. One day McKenzie was riding to an appointment when the gambler rode up and told the preacher that he had vowed to give him a whipping at the first opportunity. McKenzie turned in his saddle and said, "Sir, you have made a contract with the devil, which you are unable to fulfill." The gambler rode away.

A dancing teacher came to Clarksville and McKenzie warned his congregation against dancing. He referred to dancing masters as little puppies. This came to the ears of the teacher and when he met the preacher on the street he said, "I understand you called me a puppy." McKenzie seemed amused. He looked at the teacher a moment and said, "Yes, I did apply that appellation to your kind, but I see that I was mistaken. I will state that you appear to be a full-grown dog." Bystanders laughed and the dancing master walked away.

A district judge, drinking in a saloon, gave whisky and crackers to several lawyers who were with him, saying it was a sacrament. His action was scored from the pulpit by Dr. McKenzie. The Judge said he'd whip the preacher, and met him on the street, but McKenzie defied him, saying, "We are both public characters. You outraged propriety by your conduct and I have only done my duty to the public by denouncing your act, and I will not be humiliated by you." Friends intervened and prevented an encounter. Thirty years later Dr. McKenzie administered the real sacrament to this same judge who had repented and become a member of the church.

[*146*]

The Reverend James Graham came from Pennsylvania with his wife and his mother-in-law. Besides being a Methodist preacher he taught schools with them in Daingerfield, Clarksville and finally in Paris, the last school being Paris Female Institute that was many years an educational center for young women from a wide area. One of the Paris public free schools, built on the site of the Female Institute, is named in his honor, James Graham School.

The Reverend Anthony Travelstead lived in Paris during the years preceding the war between the sections. He was a Cumberland Presbyterian preacher and served over a wide area, going when and where he was wanted, taking as pay whatever was offered, many times taking nothing. When he was not preaching, he did carpenter work, with one of his sons who was a building contractor. He was a man of large frame and girth and had a voice to match, and when holding prayer meeting in his home in Paris might be heard on the public square four blocks distant.

Like most preachers of those days, he had an appropriate answer to questions that might be asked him in a spirit of levity. Once when he was in Clarksville a youth asked him, "Why do you pray so loud; do you think the Lord is deaf?" Grandpa, as he was familiarly called, being then along in years, said, "No, son, I don't think the Lord is deaf, but I know he is such a long way from this ungodly town."

The Reverend William Brackeen and his three stalwart sons, James, Thomas and William junior, came to the Valley in the early days and settled in what became southern Lamar County. Like other preachers of that time he had no limit to his field. When he was not going from one place to another, his Bible under his arm, a knife and maybe a pistol on his belt, a long-barreled gun over his shoulder and a blanket in which to wrap himself if night overtook him far from a house, he farmed and cleared land.

[*147*]

There were "varmints" in Sulphur bottom near the Brackeen home, and they supplied meat for the family if they were bears, and those not eatable were killed to protect the domestic animals. One day he heard a hog squealing and going toward the sound found a bear making a meal off one of his hogs. One shot brought bruin down and as the hog was past saving it was killed. Being warm weather the meat of the two could not be kept so Uncle William took it around and divided it with the neighbors.

One day while Mr. Brackeen was chopping firewood his dog went in a thicket not far from the house and presently gave forth sounds of distress. Not having his gun, Mr. Brackeen cut a club and with it and his axe went to where the dog was growling and yelping and found the animal battling with a panther. The axe and club disposed of the panther, and the preacher went back to wood cutting. He assaulted the devil in cabins and forts, sometimes as far south as the Trinity River, and when he passed away was mourned by everyone who had sat under his ministrations.

Other preachers of later days who attained prominence by their work in the Valley included the Reverend Robert C. Buckner who came from Kentucky in the late 'fifties. He served the Baptist Church in Paris several years and published a paper, "The Religious Messenger," afterwards called "The Texas Baptist." He went to Dallas where he continued publication of his paper and later established Buckner Orphans' Home, a project he had conceived and planned before he left Paris.

Elder Charles Carlton of the Christian Church was preacher and teacher for years. Carlton College in Bonham was a school that afforded education to hundreds of men and women who in adult life became leaders in business and professions over the Southwest.

CONDITIONS IN THE VALLEY were told by an Englishman, Dr. Edward Smith, who in 1849 traveled through

[148]

the Valley and other sections of Texas, looking for a location for a proposed colony of his countrymen. He made report to the promoters of the affair, covering every phase of life as he had seen it. Somewhat stilted as compared with words in use today, it is yet a true picture of that time.

He said: "In morality I believe the people rank very high. Nothing militating against this opinion was found by us" (he had as a traveling companion James Barrow, a civil engineer), "but we found them truthful, honest, hospitable and friendly to a remarkable extent. The Presbyterians, Methodists, Baptists and Episcopalians, and other sects, have extensive organizations in this part of Texas. No sect possesses any political advantage not enjoyed by the others, but the Presbyterians and Methodists are more influential than the other bodies.

"The Sabbath is much respected and the inhabitants conscientiously attend places of worship that are located within two or three miles of most every residence. Some of these places are the houses of the settlers, others are chapels exclusively appropriated to religious and educational purposes. It was pleasing to hear the song of praise arising from a knot of people gathered under the verandah of a settler's house on the Saturday evening, in what have been called the backwoods and wilds of America, and we remembered that the millions of our intelligent countrymen were then busily engaged in commerce, while these 'wild savages' were so auspiciously entering on devotions of the Sabbath.

"It was no unpleasant sight to notice the husband and wife riding a single horse to a place of worship, accompanied by their little children, riding two-by-two. A neatly built chapel, filled with well-dressed and happy-looking men and women, set in the shade of a dense wood, among the trees of which are scores of beautifully caparisoned horses awaiting the arrival of their riders, is worthy the pen of a poet or the pencil of an artist. We saw such a

[*149*]

scene on several occasions. The sermons we heard were thoroughly scriptural, if not able, and the lack of religion need not be feared in Northeast Texas.

"The most perfect security to life and property reign throughout Northeast Texas," Dr. Smith continued, "far more perfect than can be found in the other states or in Europe. We traveled alone, day and night, and never received incivility or injury. The only attempt to impose on us was by one of our own countrymen." (This referred to an Englishman in Jefferson who tried to sell them horses at a price much higher than the market when they were starting their trip.) "The inhabitants behaved very kindly to us and would not be paid for board or lodging.

"Being desirous for new settlers as their resources develop and their property increases in value, they are not likely to offer injury to those they wish to come among them. They are too rich to render theft worth their attention. Unprotected, loaded wagons, broken down on the road, have been known to be unmolested many days. They can boast of their admitted honesty in paying debts and in a legal regard for the rights and property of others.

"The law is firmly administered. Mr. Thomas, whom we visited in Hopkins County, told us he was visited by a steer that could open the door of his corn crib and eat corn which was selling for $1.25 a bushel. He could find no one who claimed to own the steer, and having heard that a steer shot through one horn would leave the place, he took his rifle and shot the steer's horn. Then an owner appeared and had Thomas indicted for shooting his animal with malicious intent. Conviction meant a term in state prison. However, the jury said there was not malicious intent, but set the damage at $4. Thomas had to pay that and the costs of both sides, amounting to $90."

Dr. Smith's observations were careful, and we may believe gave a true picture of conditions in the Valley at the time he saw it.

[150]

SOME MISSIONARIES

They taught schools and preached the Gospel.

"Men of God have always, from time to time, walked among men, and made their commission felt in the heart and soul of the commonest hearer."—Emerson

WHEN the Choctaw and Chickasaw Indians came to Indian Territory in 1832, and the years following, some missionaries came with them. They had taught schools and preached to the Indians before the move, and wanting to keep up the work, some also emigrated. Aided by the Government and the Church mission boards, they established several schools in the Valley. Those in the Choctaw Nation were conducted by Presbyterians. In the Chickasaw Nation the missionaries were Methodists.

Among the Choctaw schools were Goodland conducted by Reverend O. P. Stark, Stockbridge (Eagletown post office) by Reverend Cyrus Byington, Koonsha Female Seminary at Goodwater, with Reverend Ebenezer Hotchkin in charge, Armstrong Academy conducted by the Reverend A. G. Moffatt. Pine Ridge had the Chuhala Female boarding school under Cyrus Kingsbury, and Spencer Academy directed by Reverend A. R. Reed. The last named, with Wheelock which was first under Reverend Alfred Wright, then under John Edwards, were the best known of the schools.

In the Chickasaw Nation the Reverend J. H. Carr was at Bloomfield Female Academy, Reverend J. C. Robinson at the Manual Labor Academy for boys. These schools closed when the war between the sections came on, but some of them were resumed afterwards. Three of these preacher-teachers came to Paris, Texas, a year or two after the war ended, and two of them remained until their death. Mr. Carr bought land and built a school house in which he taught several years, Mr. Stark did the same, but in 1880 he sold his school property in Paris and returned to the Choctaw Nation and taught at Spencer Academy four years until his death.

[*153*]

When Mr. Carr was instructed to establish a school, the site selected was several miles southeast of the present city of Durant and three miles from Red River. He went to the place and his axe struck the first blow to fell the trees for logs with which to build. When he was asked where his mail was to be directed he pointed to the flower-covered ground and said "Bloomfield," and so the school was named. When the school closed because of the war impending in 1860, Mr. Carr taught a free school each morning while some of the buildings were used by the Chickasaw Battalion, attached to the Confederate Army later. Bloomfield continued as a school intermittently until 1914, when the buildings burned for the third time. It was then abandoned and the personnel moved to Ardmore and established Carter Seminary. Mr. Carr's strength of character and resourcefulness were shown when one of his children died. He made her coffin and preached her funeral.

Mrs. Robinson, when living in Paris, told her Sunday School class of an Indian wedding at the Bloomfield Academy when she was a teacher. She said, "The superintendent's wife came in where the girls were making their own dresses, sewing being one of the arts taught at the school, and said an Indian couple wanted Mr. Carr to marry them, and the girls could see the ceremony. They came in. The bride wore a faded calico dress, an old plaid shawl over her shoulders and a red cotton handkerchief over her head, and was barefooted.

"The groom wore buckskin pants with buckskin fringe at the outer seams and a linsey hunting shirt trimmed with wool yarn fringe. His hair hung to his shoulders, he wore a woolen shawl wrapped around his head which he did not remove during the ceremony and a pair of heavy cowhide boots with large spurs that rattled as he walked. Neither could speak or understand English and one girl acted as interpreter. When the questions were asked they

[154]

responded with a grunt. The girl translated 'husband and wife' into 'man and woman' which amused the other girls who understood English. The ceremony ended, the Indian grunted again and they departed."

Cyrus Kingsbury had charge of the school at Pine Ridge a few miles from Fort Towson. He was born in New Hampshire and became a missionary to the Cherokee Indians in East Tennessee and then to the Choctaws in Mississippi. He stayed in Mississippi until the last of the Choctaw Indians had followed the Trail of Tears, as the long wearisome journey to the new home was called, then he followed and continued teaching and preaching until his death in his eighty-fourth year. He and most of the other missionaries in the Territory refused to take the drastic anti-slavery position of the Mission Board, and he remained with the Choctaws when they decided to join with the Southern Confederacy. Kingsbury was of small stature and had club feet. His Indian name translated into "Limping Wolf," though he was a man of gentle character and attractive personality.

The school at Goodland under Reverend O. P. Stark grew during the ten years from 1850 to 1860, when the war compelled it to close. After the war it was a school under various managements and eventually became an Indian orphanage, the Indians living near taking the children into their homes, so they could attend school, and presently building a dormitory for them. It is now, after a hundred years, greatly enlarged and doing excellent work for Indian orphans, the only mission in existence founded for the Indians by the early missionaries. The Indian name for Goodland is "Yakni Achuckma."

The missionaries were much hampered and disturbed by the Indians' love for liquor, though not all their flocks indulged. Some did, however, and in their reports to the Indian agents at Fort Towson and Fort Smith they told of some of the bad effects of drinking. Ebenezer Hotchkin wrote from Goodwater in 1854 that some of the young men who had been temperate had been drinking. He blamed it on the doggeries at Pine Bluffs, on the south side of Red River, and mentioned that one keeper of such a place had been shot and killed by another grog seller. The details of that and its result are told in another story in this collection.

SOME EDITORS

"Were it left to me to decide whether we should have a government without newspapers, or newspapers without a government, I should not hesitate a moment to prefer the latter." —Thomas Jefferson

EDITORS came to the Valley after the pioneers had tramped down the grass, made some trails, killed some Indians and whipped the country into some law and order. They brought their little presses and began publication of papers that for long were mostly legal notices, small advertisements and professional cards, with some literary essays and verses, but with little local news. Many of the publications did not last long, changed owners frequently, and sometimes were moved to other towns.

One which was established, the first, was *The Northern Standard* published by Charles DeMorse in Clarksville. For forty-five years he edited his *Standard* while engaged in many other activities and exercised powerful influence for morality and good government.

Charles Denny Morse was born in Massachusetts and when not quite twenty years old sailed from New York with a company of volunteers to help Texas gain freedom from Mexico. The vessel was captured by a British ship and taken to the Bahamas under suspicion of piracy. The men were tried and exonerated, but the young man's name had been changed. The officer enrolling the men before trial was told that his name was Charles D. Morse. It was written down DeMorse, and Charles liked it so that he continued to use that form, eventually having it legalized by the Texas Congress.

DeMorse filled various positions with the Texas government until 1842 when the members of the Congress from Red River urged him to go to Clarksville and start a newspaper. He agreed, and with some financial assistance bought a small plant in New Orleans. In August 1842, the first issue of *The Northern Standard,* Charles DeMorse, Editor and Publisher, came from the hand press, with under the heading the motto: "Long May Our Banner Brave the Breeze—the Standard of the Free." The word

[*159*]

"Northern" was omitted from the head of the paper after about ten years. Some writers have said that it was done when the war between the sections neared, but that war was near ten years in the future when the word was omitted, and thereafter the paper was *The Standard*. It is probable that the change was made because by then Texas was increasing in population, communication was easier and the *Standard,* first published for the northern portion of the Republic and State, had widened its field and was being read and quoted from border to border of Texas.

Charles DeMorse took time out to raise and command a regiment for the Confederacy, and publication ceased briefly. There was another suspension between 1875-79, due in part to ill health of the publisher. When publication was resumed the motto was omitted from the head of the paper. After his death in 1887, the paper was published a few months by his daughter, then was discontinued. DeMorse was a lawyer and attended the courts in the Valley while editing his paper. He was a man with definite principles and convictions, who left a lasting impress on Texas education and government.

Paris had newspapers, beginning in 1844, when James Wellington Latimer began his *Western Star* which he presently sold, went to Dallas and published the Dallas *Herald.* A paper was published in Paris at intervals by various owners and under different names, until 1856 when Terrell & Peterson started the *Lamar Enquirer,* and employed Judge John T. Mills to edit it. E. J. Foster was publishing the *Frontier Patriot* with its motto: "Liberty and Union, Now and Forever, One and Inseparable—Webster." He could not stand the competition with the *Enquirer* and moved to Sherman where he called his publication the *Sherman Patriot.*

In 1859 the *Enquirer* was bought by Fred W. Miner, who changed its name to the *Paris Press* and published it until the war came on. March 4, 1861, the *Press* carried the date line and "Paris, Texas (Cotton Confederacy)" which was Miner's choice of words to describe the then existing condition, the Confederacy not having been formally organized. In an editorial referring to President Lincoln's inaugural as it was reported in the Little Rock *Democrat,* which was issued during the Arkansas secession convention, he said that it "might be incorrect and intended to influence the convention," then added, "but if true we will contribute our mite to the support of Texas in resisting to the last any effort to reconstruct the Union upon any basis which admits the right of the Federal government to use force against a seceding state. We owe no allegiance to any government save that of the Republic of Texas, unless Texas is already a member of the Cotton Confederacy."

When Texas joined the Confederacy Editor Miner made good his word and served through the war as Captain of a company. In 1865 he said he had taken the oath prescribed for reconstruction and intended to "keep it in good faith," but was no nearer admitting the right of the government to propose and enforce it than he was a month before. He added, "We don't claim the right to act in opposition to the authorities because of our private opinions. No man shall dictate to us what opinions we shall hold. We admit the power to control our actions, but not our opinions. If, in order to hold an office under a 'Democratic' government it is necessary for a man to believe in the doctrine of equality of all races and colors, we expect to continue on a back seat. Time brings changes."

Miner was born in Connecticut, went to Virginia when a youth, graduated from University of Virginia and after practice of law in Virginia a while came to Paris in 1859. He was a Democrat until after the war, when his convictions led him into the Republican Party. He was prominent in that party several years and in 1879 was made Federal District Attorney for the newly-formed Northern District of Texas.   [*161*]

John Piner was editor and publisher of *Bonham News* in the 'seventies of the last century. He was of the school that called a spade a spade and not an agricultural tool. He had opinions and voiced them through his paper on everything of interest to the people. He did not like Governor O. M. Roberts' attitude toward public education and some other matters of State policy, and for a long time he carried under the name of *The Bonham News* the line, "For the Free School System of Texas, and against Governor O. M. Roberts and all who uphold him, now, henceforth and forever."

Piner demanded cash in advance for his newspaper. One day an old subscriber came and said he failed to get his paper. Piner looked on the book and said the time was out. The old subscriber said he would not have any money until Fall and could the paper be sent him and be paid then. Piner said it could not, that *The Bonham News* wouldn't be sent to his own brother on credit, but putting his hand in his pocket he pulled out a dollar and handed it to the subscriber, saying "You can pay for the paper. You owe John Piner personally a dollar."

He was careful with the papers that came in exchange to his office and kept them arranged just-so and disliked for anyone to handle them. A man who had come to Bonham from another town came to the office every week and read the paper from his home town. He stopped coming and one day met Piner on the street and said, "I haven't been around to read the paper because I am getting it by mail." Piner said, "Yes, I sent a subscription to it for you."

John Piner detested pomposity and when a man who had been an officer in the Confederate Army came from another state to Bonham and did a good deal of strutting, Piner wrote and printed a little paragraph so plainly intended to puncture the ego of the newcomer that it could not be mistaken. The man was furious and sent a friend to Piner with a challenge to a duel. Piner read the chal-

[*162*]

lenge, laughed and wrote a reply which he then published in *The Bonham News* with the challenge note. The reply read: "Honored Sir: Your challenge to meet you in honorable but deadly combat received and respectfully declined for three reasons.

"First, I do not believe in duels.

"Second, I do not want to be shot.

"Third, I am not mad at anybody, and especially at you. If I desired your death, I would seek a lawful and easier way of bringing it about—I would simply get a feather from a peacock's tail, stick it in your hatband, and let you strut yourself to death. Most Respectfully," and his signature. There was no further offer of a duel.

Richard Peterson was an editor though not of a newspaper. He had come from Ohio to Paris in early days, served in various county and city offices during Reconstruction, accumulated considerable property and for a time published a tabloid monthly paper titled *Common Sense,* being atheistic in its content. For years he was a citizen whose lack of religious convictions did not affect his standing in the community, whose word was as good as his bond. He wrote his will on a scrap of paper, made his daughter his heir, said his funeral was to be simple, coffin to cost not more than $25, other expense not to exceed $100 and might be less, and concluded "I am an atheist (thank god), all religions are a curse. Written in my 84th year, sound in mind and body and wish to remain on top of the ground at least 16 more years to see the 100 mark. One world at a time." He died two years later, in his 86th year.

Reverend R. C. Buckner, pastor of a Baptist Church in Paris near eighty years ago, and for several years afterward, published a weekly *Religious Messenger,* and early in 1875 moved to Dallas where he presently established Buckner Orphans Home. Noting this removal in the issue of *Common Sense* for March, 1875, Mr. Peterson

[*163*]

said, "Besides ours there is a monthly, two weeklies and a daily published in this city. There was another weekly, *The Religious Messenger,* but Tophet was beginning to congeal in these parts and it absquatulated double-quick to the benighted shades of Hades, alias Dallas, where they have a gas factory to light the funeral marches to the grave."

Peterson had an only son who fell ill of a fever when a few years old and died. The doctor had put the child in ice packs and Peterson declared that was what caused death. On the child's grave marker was the date of death, in August, and the words, "Frozen to Death." The father also made this charge publicly, the doctor sued him for libel and he in turn sued the doctor for malpractice. All either got was lawyers' fees and court costs.

Some later-day editors in the Valley brightened many a moment for their readers with their quips and sallies concerning national as well as local affairs. Joe Taylor of *Clarksville Times* and Jim Lowry of *Honey Grove Signal,* weekly papers, were two of the able editors who for years entertained and instructed their readers. Lowry was an exponent of buttermilk as a drink superior to any other, while Taylor rested his case on potlicker. Lowry, like Don Quixote and the windmills, broke many a verbal lance against the iron stairs in Dallas union station, but did not live long enough to see them removed. He never solicited an advertisement nor a subscription, yet he had one of the most prosperous papers in Texas.

Joe Taylor was enticed to the *Dallas News* where for years he was conductor of the State Press column and wrote editorials that were quoted by big papers all over the country. He, too, passed away while still in his prime and at the height of his usefulness.

SOME LAWYERS

"The study of the law is useful in a variety of points of view. It qualifies a man to be useful to himself, to his neighbors and to the public."—Thomas Jefferson

AMONG early arrivals in the Valley were some lawyers who found opportunity to practice their profession, first at Jonesboro and later at the county seats as the Valley was settled and counties were created. Some of them tilled the soil in addition to practicing at the bar, some became editors, or teachers, and some were preachers on occasion.

One of the latter was John B. Denton, for whom a Texas county and city are named. Apprenticed to a blacksmith, Denton gave up the trade after his father's death and began preaching. His wife taught him to read and write. He preached in Arkansas and Texas from 1834 to 1838, then located in Clarksville and practiced law to make a living for his growing family. As a lawyer he attended court in Fannin County, and was invited to preach for the settlers the next Sunday and did so. That sermon is believed to have been the first preached in Fannin County. Denton was killed in the fight with Indians at Village Creek.

Amos Morrill was born in Massachusetts. After graduating from Boston College he went to Tennessee where he practiced law until in 1838 he came to Texas and became one of the strong men at the bar. He located in Clarksville and attended all the courts in the Valley. In 1853 the district attorney asked for a rule, disbarring Morrill, alleging unethical conduct. Judge W. S. Todd heard the testimony and decided Counsellor Morrell was guilty of "a serious impropriety" toward a client, but without venal intent. He reprimanded Morrill in open court but declined to disbar him.

Charles DeMorse's report in the "Standard" of the incident led Morrill to sue the editor-lawyer for $20,000 damages, alleging he had been libeled. The suit dragged along two years when Morrill was given a verdict for $5,000. He immediately released the judgment, except the costs, which DeMorse had to pay. In 1856 Morrill was

[*167*]

indicted in Lamar County, charged with "Using as true a counterfeit note." The district attorney, when the case was called the next year, fearing he had no case, asked for a nolle pros, but Morrill demanded a jury, was tried and acquitted. Then he was charged with perjury, demanded and was given trial, and was acquitted on that count. Soon after his experience in the Lamar County District Court he went to Austin. He practiced law there until 1867, when he was appointed by the military authority one of the five judges of Texas Supreme Court, and was by the other members chosen as presiding judge. In 1872 he was named to the Federal bench for Eastern District of Texas when he was 63 years old and filled that position a number of years.

W. M. (Buckskin) Williams was an early comer from Virgina and served as district attorney when Lamar County's first district court was held in 1841. He afterwards served Texas in various responsible positions. John M. Hansford was District Judge and while he did not live in the Valley he spent some time holding court in the four counties fronting the river. A Texas county was named in his honor.

The Fowler brothers, A. J. and Brad, who had been at Jonesboro earlier, came to Lamar County and practiced law, and in the 'fifties others were Henry Woodsworth, J. M. Morphis and J. S. Gillett. Born in Kentucky, Gillett was reared in Missouri, fought in the war with Mexico and after that settled in Paris. He was elected to the Legislature in 1846 and after that service moved to Austin and became a Texas ranger. He was adjutant general under Sam Houston, then moved to Lampasas and died in 1874. His son, James B., entered Ranger service when 19 and after seven years was made chief of police in El Paso when the railroads reached that town, retired several years later and became a cattle rancher.

John T. Mills followed Hansford on the District Bench

[168]

and served eight years, then became a newspaper editor in Paris. He, also, was honored by having a Texas county named for him.

It is difficult to classify Sam Bell Maxey, who besides being distinguished in the Mexican war was a profound lawyer and a successful Major General in the Confederate Army, and who became a United States Senator after his political disability was removed by personal order of President Grant, with whom he had served in Mexico. He came to Paris in 1857, and was a citizen of Texas until his death. He was engaged in some of the greatest cases in the history of the Texas bar.

William B. Wright, born in Georgia, graduated from Princeton when 17 years old, studied law with Georgia's Chief Justice, John H. Lumpkin and was admitted to practice in the Supreme Court of that state when 19. In 1854 he came to Paris, Texas and became a leader at that bar. Elected to the Confederate Congress he was chairman of the committee on Indian Affairs and negotiated treaties with the Choctaw and Chickasaw Indians for the Confederacy. At the end of his term he was made a Major on the staff of President Jefferson Davis, serving until the surrender. After the war ended he lived in Clarksville and practiced in partnership with Judge Marshall Sims, then returned to Paris in 1873 and was elected a member of the Constitutional Convention, and had a large part in framing the Constitution which Texas now has.

As a criminal lawyer he was considered one of the greatest in the South, engaged as counsel for 92 cases where murder was charged, and never lost a case. In the early 'seventies he had a series of cases such as no other attorney ever had. He secured acquittal of a man named Henderson, charged with murder of an old man named McFeeland, later cleared Pomp Duty for killing Henderson, and still later cleared Matt Harris for killing Pomp Duty. He moved to San Antonio in 1888, engaged in banking and

[169]

the law, and passed away in 1895, having made a record perhaps never equalled.

Henry D. McDonald was a lawyer who for near fifty years was active in practice and prominent in Texas. He was a son of Dr. Henry G. McDonald, who had been a surgeon in United States Army, and came to Texas in 1837, settling in southern Lamar County. Henry had his early education at McKenzie school near Clarksville, and when just past his majority was admitted to the bar in Paris, in October, 1868, being given his "certificate of good character" (which was required in those days) by Justice G. W. DeWitt of Lamar County. In 1886 he was elected to the State Senate where he was chairman of Judiciary Committee No. 1, and president pro tem. He was counsel in many important cases during his practice and had retired several years before his death in 1925. His wife was a daughter of Colonel W. B. Wright.

Reuben R. Gaines, Alabama born, became a lawyer in his native state and practiced until the war began. He left his office to become a member of Third Alabama Cavalry. In 1866 he came to Red River County and ten years later was elected district judge, under the new Texas Constitution. He moved to Paris, served two terms, and two years later was elected associate justice, Texas Supreme Court. Reelected twice he was then made Chief Justice. He was counted one of the greatest jurists in Texas history.

Henry W. Lightfoot came to Paris in June, 1872. He had enlisted in Forrest's Cavalry, Confederate Army, when 16 and served through the war. He was prominent not only in the Valley but over the State. He was counsel for Land Commissioner W. L. McGaughey in 1893 and secured acquittal in impeachment before Texas Senate. The Fifth Supreme Judicial District Court was created that year, and Governor J. S. Hogg named Lightfoot to the place of Chief Justice. He was elected to the position, but resigned after four years and returned to private practice. He

[*170*]

passed away in Alaska in 1901, where he had gone on legal business.

When James M. Long came back from the Confederate Army, leaving one leg on Shiloh battle field, he began to read law and was admitted to practice. Being a one-legged man (we call them amputees since the second world war) he had the sympathy of the people of Lamar County and they gave him some business. He held several county offices at different times, having been presiding judge of the county court, district clerk, and county attorney two separate terms. He was self-named Private Jim Long, in a time when there was a plethora of captains, majors and colonels in politics. He was not a great lawyer, but he knew the groundwork of the law and did very well in the average small case. He had a scrap book, largely clippings of incidents connected with the war then not so many years in the past, and he used this rather successfully in reading to juries when defending a man who was charged with a misdemeanor. Private Long was a figure in the courts of Lamar County many years.

When he was about seventy years old Moman Pruiett began writing a book, which was published in Oklahoma City, where he then lived, with the title, "Moman Pruiett, Criminal Lawyer." For more than forty years his voice had been heard in court houses in the Valley, in the Pacific Northwest, and in Florida, generally in defense of men and women charged with murder. During that time he, alone or with associate counsel, defended 343 persons charged with murder, and 303 were acquitted by juries. Only one was sentenced to hang, and Pruiett went to Washington and secured a commutation to imprisonment for life from President McKinley.

Pruiett was born in 1872, and when yet a child was a bootblack, horse holder and errand runner in Fayetteville, Arkansas. His parents followed the construction of the St. Louis and San Francisco Railroad through Arkansas in the

[171]

'eighties, the father supplying meat for the construction gangs most of the time. When the Frisco reached Paris, Texas, Moman and his parents came also and the Pruietts had a small boarding house, while the boy swept the offices of a law firm and read some of the books. In Arkansas he had been sentenced to the penitentiary for forgery and served six months when about sixteen years old. Some time after arriving in Paris he was charged with robbery from the person of a drunken man and went to Texas penitentiary for five years. His mother's pleas persuaded Governor Charles Culberson to pardon him after two years and he returned to Paris and continued reading law books.

In the lawyers' office one day he heard them discussing a case in which they had been retained, and suggested to them that he had seen high court decisions bearing on similar cases, which they had not found. They used them to get an acquittal for their client. He was working for Ambrose Long, manager of a cotton weighing yard, who had given the youth employment when he heard no one else would do so because he was a convict. While Pruiett was passing the hotel one evening in 1895 Judge David E. Bryant, then holding a term of Federal Court in Paris, was sitting in front of the hotel and stopped him.

Judge Bryant had been told by Stilwell Russell, a prominent lawyer from Dallas who was attending the court session, that the Pruiett youth was a better lawyer than many licensed practitioners, and Judge Bryant had heard from other men that Pruiett was probably not guilty of the robbery charge, though there had been some evidence against him. Judge Bryant talked with Moman a while, handed him a $20 bill and told him to come up to his court when he could get off from work, and to use the money to buy a suit of clothes. Pruiett did so, and when the afternoon session of Judge Bryant's court was about to close he called the youth to the bench, told the clerk to swear Moman Pruiett as an attorney and officer of the court and to

[172]

let the minutes show that it was done on motion of the Judge. From that time Pruiett was busy forty years keeping criminals out of prison or from the gallows or electric chair.

Pruiett went to Oklahoma a few years later, and when courts were established there by the Congress he found more calls for his services than he could answer. He received large fees, wasted his money gambling and drinking and spending lavishly, and when he began writing his book was living on the Oklahoma State pension of $40 a month, with an occasional small case in the minor courts.

The book he wrote told of his prison record, of his work as a child and a youth, gave details of many of the cases in which he was counsel, and told of Judge David Bryant making him an officer of his Court. Soon after the book was published Judge Randolph Bryant read it and asked Pruiett to come to Paris at his next term of court. The records of the Federal Court in Paris had burned in the fire of March 21, 1916, and Randolph Bryant called Pruiett before the bench, had the oath re-administered to him so it would be on the record with the notation that it was done by order of the Court himself. Less than two years later Moman Pruiett passed away. The boy who had ten months common schooling and thirty months in penal institutions, had made a reputation as a "Criminal Lawyer" never equalled so far as any record shows.

JOHN T. MILLS — POLITICIAN

"The conduct of a wise politician is ever suited to the present posture of affairs."—Plutarch

John T. Mills, finishing his fourth term, eight years as Judge of the District which included the Valley counties in Texas, was a candidate for Governor of Texas in 1849, when George T. Wood was a candidate for re-election. The third candidate, Peter Hansborough Bell, was elected. Mills had been a district judge under the Republic, when the judges sitting together composed the Supreme Court, and was appointed one of the eight district judges when the Republic became a State of the Union.

Less than two years after he was elected district judge, Mills was married in Red River County. The record dated July 9, 1843, says, "Before William B. Stout, Chief Justice of Red River County, appeared John T. Mills, Wade H. Vining, his wife, Martha Vining, and their daughter, Mary Jane, and entered into this indenture: 'That for and in consideration of the love and affection cherished by the said John T. toward the said Mary Jane, and in full consideration of the promise of Mary Jane, by and with the approbation of her parents, to unite herself in marriage to the said John T., as well as the further consideration of $1 to John T. paid by Wade H., the said John T., by this indenture, doth bargain, sell, alien and convey unto the said Mary J., her heirs, etc., all right, title, interest which the said John T. has in and to a certain tract of land 640 acres, in Lamar County, south of Sulphur, located by a land warrant issued to John Mott from the War Department of Texas, December 23, 1841.'"

In addition to this land, John T. gave to Mary Jane, "for her sole use and benefit and behoof, the following described Negroes, slaves for life: Ephraim, a boy now about 18 years old, dark complexion; Grace, a woman about 26 and her infant about 2 years old; Jane, a woman about 25 and her infant about 2 years old." In addition John T. held himself indebted to the said Mary J. in "the sum of

[177]

$5,000, good and lawful money of this Republic," for which he gave her a lien on all real estate he might own in case he should "depart this life before the said Mary J."

For her part, Miss Vining promised that in consideration of the conveyance of lands and slaves, "as well as for the love and affection she hath for the said John T., agrees and stipulates that on the third day of August, 1843, she will become the wife of the said John T."

Wade H. Vining was district clerk of Red River at this time. The marriage was solemnized and ended only by the death of Mrs. Mills at a date not given, but some time in the late 'fifties. She is buried in the Old Cemetery in Paris the stone over her grave stating only that it covers the remains of "Mary J., wife of John T. Mills," with no dates. Judge Mills had moved to Paris soon after his unsuccessful campaign for the governorship, and for a time edited a newspaper.

The judge apparently spent some money in his campaign and had sold some land to get it. Soon after he moved to Paris he executed an instrument, recorded in Lamar County, to the effect that he, in consideration by the releasing of his wife, Mary J. Mills, of all her interest in 640 acres of land located in Hopkins County (Hopkins had been cut off of Lamar in 1846), the same land he had dowered Mary Jane Vining, which land was valued at $1,280 ($2 an acre) and which he added "I had already sold to Thomas Jefferson Craft but which was the sole property of my wife," the said John T. Mills bargained and sold to his wife, to be her separate property, a mulatto boy, slave for life, named Sam, about nine years old, and a Negro girl, about seven years old, named Harriet. The instrument set no value on the slaves, but Mrs. Mills was no doubt satisfied they were worth at least as much as the land.

Two Englishmen, Edward Smith and John Barrow, who traveled through a part of the Valley in 1849, looking at

[178]

land for a proposed colony, met Judge Mills when they were in Paris, and he gave them a glowing account of what the Valley would be when the Great Pacific Rail Road was built and which was then being talked of. Later they ran onto him in Dallas, and from their description he used just about the same electioneering methods that are in use by some candidates today.

The Englishmen said other business kept them from hearing Judge Mills address the voters in Dallas, but afterwards he told them he had freely expressed his sentiments on the subject of the railroad which he advocated passing through Texas rather than west from St. Louis. One of the Englishmen added:

"To show the offhand character of Texas politics, the scene we witnessed at Alexander's store on first entering the town that morning is sufficiently characteristic. The Judge was taking his ease in a reclining position on the counter, a motley group was assembled, sitting in the various attitudes on nail barrels, stools, grocery casks and other articles scattered with some degree of order through the store. Every man was chewing the native weed. Conversation of a lively nature on various topics seemed to engage the party on our arrival, interspersed with which were some political posers to the Judge, who would reply to them by a sally of wit which set the company in a roar of laughter, his Honor being one of the sort who love a joke. Our business soon became the interesting topic, and gratuitous advice flowed from their lips as to what ought be our course of procedure, the tendency of which implied that the neighboring country was the most advantageous in the State for a body of Englishmen to settle on."

HOME LIFE IN THE VALLEY

"The custom and fashion of today will be the awkwardness and out-rage of tomorrow—so arbitrary are these transient laws."—Dumas

Going to Market
Laundering and Soap Making
Two Styles of Beds
Sermons Were Long
Dress and Hair Fashions
Candles for Illumination
Death and Burials

LIFE WENT VERY WELL in the Valley in the late 'fifties, the years before the men went to war, a conflict that changed the course of events and outmoded most of the manners and customs of those pleasant times. Life in Paris, Texas, was doubtless much like it was in other towns, so let the description by a twelve-year-old boy serve as the chronicle—a boy who had good eyes and ears, who saw and heard everything and had opinions or reached conclusions on all subjects. This is the story that boy told me, when he was past 75 years old:

"Father called me early one morning, having told me we would go to market, and while I was dressing, I heard a horn blowing. We went to the northeast corner of the square, the horn blowing at intervals, where was a wide board laid on trestles, a big man behind it. On the board was a half a beef and a stack of rough straw paper such as was used in the stores. The big man cut off the beef in chunks of a size to suit the customer and wrapped it in the paper, using no twine for there was none. When the meat was taken home the cook had to slice it and put it in the skillet.

"We could always tell when the neighbors were up in the morning by the sound of steak being beaten on a board with a hammer to break the fiber and 'tender' it. Then we could hear coffee mills, nailed to the wall of the kitchen, the grinding heard for some distance. Coffee was bought green in the bean, taken home and parched in a shallow pan in the oven of the stove, and watched closely so it would not burn. Coffee was the universal drink, little tea being used, and was bought by most families by the sack. Between the steak pounding and the coffee mills, one could tell the town was coming to life.

"Then rather often a neighbor would come in to borrow enough coffee for breakfast, having neglected to get a supply the day before. Or it might be to borrow a chunk of fire, or a pan of coals, to start a fire which had not been properly banked at night. Matches were a scarce article, and not much account, being tipped with sulphur and sometimes igniting in the box in hot weather. Sugar was a dark brown wet substance and sticky.

"Going to market we passed the store of John Broad on the north side of the square. He was one of the most re-markable and best men of the town. At his place he sold candy, fruit, home-baked gingerbread, of which one could get a big slice and a glass of corn 'beer' for a dime. No nickels were in use then; everything, even an apple, was a dime. In front of this store was a barrel of tar for team-sters to lubricate the wooden spindles of their 'tar-pole' wagons.

"There were no washboards, nor wringers. The gar-ments were put in a kettle of boiling water, soaped and laid on a heavy board or flat stone and beat with paddles by the Negro women. The soap was homemade. Every home had an ash hopper, a wooden trough set on legs into which the wood ashes from the fireplace were put and water poured on, which percolated into a bucket. The lye thus made was put in an iron kettle with bones, fats, any kind of grease, and the result was what was called soft soap and was fine for laundering.

"Most people raised gourds, of many sizes and shapes. They were used, if large, as a jug to carry water, or cut in halves to hold a supply of soft soap. Those with long stems and small bowls were cut in half and used for dippers, much preferred to metal dippers in taking a drink of water from the bucket that hung on the back porch to keep as cool as possible, for there was no ice. The water in the soft wood buckets always tasted of wood, but people who could afford them bought cedar buckets with brass hoops, which were kept shined and of which they were very proud.

"When Fall came hogs were butchered, hung up to cool

[*184*]

overnight, cut into joints, sides and ribs next day, the fat rendered into lard, and the trimmings laid on a thick plank and chopped with a hatchet as fine as possible, for sausage. There were no meat or vegetable grinders other than those put in our mouths by nature, nor were there sewing machines, all sewing being done by hand.

"There were two styles of beds—slats and ropes. There were no bed springs nor factory-made mattresses. The slat bed had narrow boards laid across the bedstead and on them the tick was laid. It was so-called from the 'ticking' of which it was made, a bag the size of the bed filled with corn shucks, or straw. On top of this one put another tick filled with feathers, down plucked from geese if possible, or chicken or duck feathers if the down was not obtainable. Those who were really affluent generally had two of these feather ticks, which made the bed pretty high but that was what was preferred.

"The rope or cord beds had, instead of slats, a rope passed through holes bored in the frame of the bed, or passed around pegs set in the frame, drawn as tight as possible and crisscrossed to make a support for the ticks. This made a good place for bedbugs, but the cords were not so hard on one's bones when the tick was thin."

This boy attended school and Sunday School and preaching. He said: "There were three churches—Baptist, Methodist and Presbyterian. The Baptists had a large frame church, of which the Reverend R. C. Buckner was pastor. They had a large congregation and the strong sermons at the revivals kept the 'sawdust trail' well filled. The Presbyterians read the sermon and it was long, under one and a half hours being thought rather brief. The longer they were, the more pleasing comment from the grownups. But us children, who had attended Sunday School from 9 until 10 o'clock, had to sit and listen until 12:30 and sometimes one o'clock on the whole duty of man.

"The Baptist and Methodist sermons were briefer and

[185]

more extempore. All had congregational singing. There were no choirs, but some leader, and he usually struck a tuning fork on the back of a pew to get the pitch of voice.

"To offset the churches the town had several racing stables, where the blanketed horses were walked around on a vacant lot near the barn to exercise them. There were race tracks at the edge of town, owned by Tom Holmes and Captain Bill Powers. Before I was old enough to understand I heard the Presbyterian minister 'read them out' of the church. The Presbyterians did not countenance gambling or horseracing."

The women's fashions were also noticed by this boy. He said: "The hoopskirt craze struck them. Hoops fastened to tapes, the hoops increasing in size from the waist down, were worn under the dress which had to be very wide. They were fastened around the waist, not always too securely and sometimes came loose. When this happened on the street it was a tragedy unless other women were present, in which case they would gather around the victim and protect her from view while repairs were made.

"The steel hoops were almost prohibitive in price and those not able to afford them made underskirts with many tucks through which pieces of rattan were slipped. They answered the same purpose as the steel and tape contraptions, but had to be laundered. If so many garments had not been worn there would sometimes have been embarrassment, for if one sat down in church without lifting the back of the skirt the front would be elevated, hiding the face of the victim from the preacher. The wearing of pantalettes, however, prevented this mishap being a tragedy.

"After the hoopskirts came the bustle, and the larger it was the more stylish. They caused the wearers to take front seats in church, so they could be seen walking up the aisle. The skirt had a train or trail dragging the ground which served principally as a street sweeper. The next 'decora-

[186]

tion' was the chignon, a bunch of material representing hair, fastened to the back of the head. The larger the bundle, the more stylish. Also there were some things called 'rats' which were small rolls of material tapering at the ends, pinned under the hair to make it stand up high on the head. This changed to bangs and frizzes, and artificial ones were sometimes worn to keep from burning the hair with hot curling irons.

"Until the time of the war bonnets were worn by old and young. They were usually of straw, some of fine quality, adorned with flowers. Some were of silk or satin with splits of wood inserted to stiffen them. Many ladies wore and boasted of their handmade bonnets.

"The churches, stores and residences were lighted with tallow or sperm candles. Ministers announced service, this evening or tomorrow evening 'at early candle lighting'. The churches were lighted with candles in cheap candlesticks and tin reflectors on each side of the preacher. People could and did sometimes make their own candles, of tallow in tin candle molds. If a large family, using many candles, a whole day might be devoted to the making, putting in the wicks, pouring the hot melted tallow, then cooling and extracting the greasy things. Sperm candles were bought at the store and were firmer than tallow. The candle trade was just as staple as sugar and coffee. In the stores the candles were carried from counter to counter in small tin candle holders.

"When there was a death the corpse was carried to the grave on a bier, the coffin setting on a framework that was carried by four or six men. There were no hearses, no undertakers, no caskets. Any good carpenter would make the coffin. Some were just painted black, some made of black walnut, and some more pretentious were covered with black velvet. Everybody knew everybody else, and would be informed of any serious illness, so if a saw and hammer was heard in the night it was known that there had been a death. [187]

"The coffins had white metal screws and handles, more for ornament than for use, and were ornate according to the social standing of the family. The grave was dug to regulation depth, then in the bottom was dug a chamber the shape and size of the coffin, which was wider where the elbows of the dead person rested. The coffin was lowered by ropes into this chamber and short boards were laid over it to keep the loose earth from falling on the coffin. The minister, mourners and friends stood about the grave, which was then filled by the friends taking turns handling the shovels. Many of the best of this earth have been laid away in this simple way.

"There were no separate lots in the old graveyard but the graves were dug here or yonder. A stranger in the town ran amuck after too much drinking and began to chase an inoffensive man who grabbed an axe as he passed a woodpile by one of the stores near the square, turned and struck his pursuer over the heart, killing him instantly. A grave was dug for his burial, near the fence of the graveyard. At about the depth it was usual to dig, the end of another decaying coffin was disclosed, so it was deemed deep enough.

"The body in a plain pine coffin was taken to the grave on a bier, and for some reason was opened before burial. Some of us boys were standing around and saw a man draw back the shroud that was used in all funerals. A great gash was seen where the axe had entered the man's breast and severed his heart. The coffin was resting on a bier and as the wound was exposed someone stumbled against the frail bier and it set the head of the dead man shaking from side to side as if in protest of the ceremonies. Let me try to tell how fast the ground passed under our bare feet. Our curiosity was entirely satisfied."

RECONSTRUCTION
and the Freedmen's Bureau

"One of the never solved enigmas of life is the number of people that bear a commission from no one, who, as a rule, are least informed on the principles of government, but who insist on exercising the powers of government to make their neighbors live the lives they desire to prescribe for them." —*Oscar W. Underwood*

RECONSTRUCTION, as the victorious Federal Congress and cabinet denominated their sending of hordes of robbers on the South after Lee's surrender, was painful, to put it mildly, and as might have been expected resulted in the KKK and other means of protection by the people.

Agents for the Freedmen's Bureau were sent to every county seat, with a bunch of soldiers to enforce their decrees. One sent to Paris, DeWitt C. Brown, he signed himself, came in 1866. He took possession of a store building and removed and appointed county and city officers at will. He adjusted debts, taking a rakeoff for the Bureau (though it is doubtful the Bureau ever got the money) and sent people to jail often without the form of a trial.

His most outrageous act was the imprisonment of Hi Duff, who owned a 200-acre farm several miles from Paris. Duff was charged with four cases of rape and two of assault and battery, and Brown took charge, tried Duff on all six cases at one sitting, and fined him $300. As Duff could not pay he threatened to keep him in jail indefinitely, but said if Duff and his wife would execute to him a deed of trust on the farm he would call it square. Duff did this under duress, and in January, 1868, the fine still not having been paid, Brown sold the farm to one M. L. Faulkner, who had accompanied him to Paris and was employed in the Bureau.

Brown began paying attention to a widow who lived in the country and had considerable property. One night, returning from a visit to the widow, as he rode through a piece of woods he was met by a KKK patrol. Brown jumped from his horse and escaped through the woods, which was as good as the KKK wanted. Next day he and Faulkner left Paris, and the Bureau presently ceased. In 1871 Duff brought suit to have the deed to Faulkner can-

[*191*]

celed, and after hearing the testimony a jury in district court gave him a verdict and cleared his title.

While the soldiers were in Paris they committed a cold-blooded murder. Wirt Smith, a young lawyer, had enlisted in the Confederate Army and at the end of the war was a captain. He had an office before the war in the second story of the store building that had been taken over by Brown. His scanty office furniture was left there when he went to war, and on his return he went to the place to get a table and the soldiers refused to let him have it. Smith protested and was shot on the sidewalk. There was nothing people could do, except what the KKK did, and it worked.

Reconstruction was not all tragedy, however. There were some humorous incidents, such as the sale of Confederate notes by Wood Shearon. John Taul had a restaurant and saloon in Paris, and in 1868 it was reported he would buy Confederate money. Some people held on to the belief that one day it would be worth something, if not its face value, so the announcement caused some interest. Mr. Shearon was a prominent citizen and had been well-to-do until the war broke him. He went into Taul's place saying he had heard Mr. Taul would buy Confederate money. Asked what he would pay for it, Taul replied that he would pay "$2.50 per hundred."

Mr. Shearon said he would bring down some and next day had a neighbor youth to help him count $30,000 in the notes, bundle it and carry it for him to Taul's place. Arrived there Mr. Shearon said he had brought some money and Taul told his son, young John, to weigh it. Mildly interested at this Mr. Shearon asked why it was to be weighed. Taul replied, " So I will know how much to pay you. I am paying $2.50 per 100 pounds. I am using it to paper a room in my home."

In Clarksville a Freedmen's Bureau was established and when the word got around the Negroes were jubilant—

[*192*]

they were going to get something for nothing. A few miles from town lived John Ford, an industrious farmer who had lost his slaves by the war. One day soon after the Bureau was established, one of his former slaves came to him and asked for the loan of a wagon and team, as he had to go to town to get his bureau. Ford wondered where the Negro had gotten money to buy a piece of furniture and said, "I did not know you had bought a bureau." The Negro said, "No, sir, I ain't bought one. They tells me the soldiers in town has one for every colored man, and I want to go get mine." Ford smiling told him he was welcome to the wagon and team, which the Negro drove joyfully away, but returned bitterly disappointed.

Many of the Negroes refused to change their fealty to the white men who had treated them well and cared for them. When Peter Madrey came to Bonham in the early years he brought Ben, a youthful Negro slave, who stayed in Bonham when freed and became known as Old Ben, liked and respected by every white man who knew him. But some of the Negroes in Bonham, as elsewhere, behaved as if they owned the town and it was necessary for the KKK to operate.

After one visit to an obstreperous Negro, complaint was made to the Bureau, and a squad of soldiers from Sherman came to Bonham, arrested several Bonham men and took them and some Negroes as witnesses to Sherman. Among the witnesses, or expected witnesses, was Old Ben. Warned to tell the truth or he would be shot, Ben was sworn by the Bureaucrat and asked if he knew a Bonham man named White Ragsdale. Old Ben thundered, "You are mighty right." Then he was asked what kind of man Ragsdale was and Ben said loudly, "He's a white man."

Ben's attitude angered the officer, and he warned Ben to be more respectful; that saying a man was a white man did not tell the kind of citizen he was. He asked what character Ragsdale was, and Ben replied, "Mr. Ragsdale is a

[193]

white man, and you're mighty right, he's a good one." Ben admitted knowing about the KKK visit but not about who was there. He said, "You're mighty right. I don't know Mr. Ragsdale was there." That ended the hearing.

SOON AFTER THE WAR between the sections ended, Albion W. Tourgee, a lawyer and writer, came South to reform the people, as did many others. He went back after a time and wrote a story which he titled, "A Fool's Errand, by One of the Fools." He apparently realized the South did not need reforming, but asked only to be let alone.

To the Valley during that period came a family of four, C. C. Granger, his wife, son and daughter. They stopped in Paris, and Granger built a frame house in that part of town where the former slaves were settling and began a school for Negroes. Some of the Negroes attended, others looked askance at the white man putting himself on an equality with them socially.

One night a gang of young white men persuaded Granger to go with them to raid a watermelon patch. Melons were plentiful and to be had almost for the asking, but it was thought to be sport to get them the other way. The game was to take a green hand and when he got in the melon patch one or two members of the gang would begin shooting, supposedly at the thieves, the others would run, and the green hand usually made the best speed. It was an old game in those days. In this instance, one of the men with a gun, whether by design or accident, fired at so low an angle that one shot struck Granger in one eye and destroyed the sight. Thereafter Granger did not attempt to fraternize with the white people, presently the school wasted away, then he died and the others of the family moved away. They had come on a Fool's Errand.

WHEN THE RAILROADS CAME

"These railroads—could but the whistle be made musical and the rumble and the jar got rid of—are positively the greatest blessings that the ages have wrought for us." —*Hawthorne*

MORE THAN FIFTY YEARS passed after Claiborne Wright and his family settled on Red River before railroads came to the Valley to take the place of the river and its boats as carriers of the products of the Valley to market, and to bring in the supplies that were needed by the increasing population.

The first effort to build a road was in 1853, when the charter for the Memphis, El Paso & Pacific Rail Road was granted by the Texas Legislature to a group of men of Bowie, Red River, Lamar and Fannin Counties. The road was to run from the Arkansas state line westward along the divide between Red and Sulphur Rivers in those counties, and on to El Paso. It was not until 1856 that the survey was made, from six miles west of the Arkansas state line, 224 miles, into Wise County. Some grading on the first ten miles was done, but not enough to meet the terms of the charter. Renewal was granted and some additional grading was done, but the war between the sections came on and everything stopped.

South of the Valley the Southern Pacific was building from the Louisiana state line through Marshall, and the Houston & Texas Central was headed north, having a line to Millican by the time the war came on. When the war ended these two lines resumed building but the MEP&P was still unable to finance.

Z. B. Tyler was chief engineer of the MEP&P, and died in 1862, while an officer in a Confederate artillery company. His executor found among his papers a draft issued to Tyler, $450, and it being unpaid the executor brought suit against the railroad for the payment, in 1868, the war having prevented earlier action. Judgment for the note, with interest, was given, and execution given Sheriff John Bland of Lamar County. The sheriff levied on everything the road might have or lay claim to, advertised a sale

[197]

and sold it to Enoch L. Fancher for $3,000, made deed and paid the judgment besides two other judgments, and $16.75, costs of suit.

In 1870, the Texas Legislature granted a charter to some Eastern capitalists under the name of Southern Transcontinental Rail Road on the same line surveyed and partly graded for the MEP&P. Enoch L. Fancher was one of the incorporators and had bought the MEP&P for his company at a nominal price. The Southern Pacific, which had been renamed the Texas & Pacific, was building toward Dallas from Marshall, the Houston and Texas Central was coming toward Sherman, and the Missouri, Kansas & Texas was building through Indian Territory to a junction with the Central. The Valley was about to get railroads.

The Transcontinental began building from Texarkana and Sherman and by 1873 had come into Lamar County from the west, stopping ten miles from Paris when the panic of 1873 dried up the financial sources. The gap between the two parts of this road, which had become a part of the Texas & Pacific, was closed in 1876, giving a line from Texarkana to Sherman.

The survey of the MEP&P had not gone to Sherman or Bonham, but had turned southwest after passing Honey Grove. When the Transcontinental took over the right-of-way it tried to make Clarksville and Paris give a bonus for having the line come through the towns. This was prevented by Senator E. L. Dohoney of Paris who fostered a bill requiring the Transcontinental to follow the survey without any bonus from the towns on the line. Bonham was not so lucky. The survey of the MEP&P did not reach Bonham, but the Transcontinental knew the Katy and Central were to meet at or near Sherman, so it altered its line from west of Honey Grove, to go to Sherman through Bonham. The Galveston News in 1873 said Bonham had donated to the railroad $26,000, the depot to be south of the court

[198]

house. There were no details of what authority promised the money, but it apparently was not paid, for in 1877 the Galveston News said the railroad had sued the City of Bonham for the money promised it for running its line through that City. If the railroad got anything it is not of record. It is doubtful that the City promised a bonus, as it would have no authority to do so, and it was doubtless private subscriptions such as Paris and other cities later paid to other railroads for coming into their corporate limits.

The Missouri, Kansas & Texas, better known as the Katy, was the first railroad to bridge Red River in the Valley. Its first train ran into Denison the evening of Christmas Day, 1872, and Denison was for some time the terminus of the road. The Houston & Texas Central was almost there and early in 1873 connection of the two roads was made, so that a train carrying U. S. soldiers into Texas to quell an Indian uprising in the western part of the Territory and along the Texas border, could go part way down the Central.

The second railroad into Paris was the St. Louis and San Francisco from Fort Smith, Arkansas, which arrived in 1887. Construction had been made from both north and south, the bridge built over Red River north of Paris, the second across the river in the Valley. Connection was made about fifty miles north of Paris while a train from the north waited, then came into Paris the afternoon of May 14, 1887.

Getting these railroads through Indian Territory required some lobbying. There had to be an act of the Congress, a permit from the War Department to bridge the river as it was theoretically navigable, and finally an act from the Indian Nations through which the lines passed.

Some Paris men had good friends in Choctaw Nation through which the Frisco was surveyed, and worked with the railroad officials to get the Indian permit. There was some opposition among members of the Choctaw Council, so a number of them were invited to take a trip and see a railroad. They were taken across country to the Katy, then into Denison, and there they were "entertained" to such an extent and in such manner that the permit was readily voted when the Indian Council took up the application.

Other railroads have come into the Valley since then, and all served to increase the population and the business of the people. Towns were built along the lines, and villages through which they passed became towns, some growing into cities.

Besides lobbying it took money to get most of the railroads, as they usually asked payment of a "bonus" from towns through which they proposed to build. Paris paid $35,000 for the Frisco, subscribed by individuals, and about as much for other roads later. This in addition to right-of-way and depot grounds, but it was considered worth the cost to have rail transportation in a day when horses and buggies were the only means of personal travel and mule teams or oxen were the power for transporting merchandise.

The river had served its purpose, but it flows today as in the years gone by, though it is not called on to give the service it gave then.

"THE TRAIL OF TEARS"

*"And, though their hearts were sad at
   times and their bodies were weary
Hope still guided them on. . . ."*
                              —Longfellow

TRIBAL GOVERNMENT

*Tribal laws of early days provided
penalties for misdeeds, rather than
commands for doing what some
might have thought should be done.*

REMOVAL OF TWELVE THOUSAND Choctaw Indians from Mississippi and Alabama to the lands given in exchange for their original area was a masterpiece of bungling in a physical sense. The original intention was to bring them from Memphis and Vicksburg in steamboats up the Arkansas and Red Rivers. While the emigrants were being gathered for these embarkation points a Washington bureau decided it would be cheaper to transport them all the way by wagons, despite the fact that there were no roads fit for travel. Also it was offered that Indians who walked all the way would be fed along the route and be given $10 each in cash. The wagons broke down along the road and the result was that those who survived the "Trail of Tears" arrived footsore and hungry, leaving many dead and buried on the way.

Entering the territory set aside for them, some of the Indians stopped a few miles inside the eastern boundary, about one-third went north to the Canadian, Poteau and Arkansas River valleys, and some went west to where now is Bryan County. At their first stopping place the Reverend Alfred Wright, who had been a missionary to the Choctaws in the original homes, and who followed them to the Territory, established a church and school. There was a spring supplying water, and the Choctaws cleared land for the church and school and some for growing corn. Two church buildings were erected as the years passed and in 1845 a stone church house was built that stands today, after more than one hundred years. The church and school was called Wheelock, and nearby now is a school bearing the same name.

Not far from Wheelock was the home of the principal chief of the Choctaws, Thomas LeFlore, who had succeeded Greenwood LeFlore who incurred the dislike of some of the Indians and who went back to Mississippi.

Later Basil LeFlore was principal chief and had his home a few miles southwest of where now is Hugo in Choctaw County.

The Chickasaws were given lands west of the Choctaws, which included what is now Bryan County and some of the counties north of it. Both tribes, soon after arrival, set up tribal governments, chose their legislators or councils, and made laws for government of their people. The Chickasaws established the capital at Tishomingo and the Choctaws held councils at various places, finally selecting Tushkahoma where a brick council house was built.

The two nations divided their areas into counties which existed until statehood, in each of which there was a court ground and at least one building, and gradually settlements grew into villages and a few towns, as traders were permitted to come into the Territory and some white men came and intermarried with the Indians.

The laws were as well enforced as those of the white men in the states, better in some places. The punishment for murder, criminal assault or a second conviction for horsetheft was death by shooting. For petty larceny the penalty was not more than 39 lashes with a hickory withe and for grand larceny not more than 100 lashes on the bare back. Having no jails then, the only punishments were death or whipping, and at each court ground there was a whipping tree which the offenders embraced, with guards holding their arms around the tree while another laid on the lashes.

The very earliest laws regulated marriages and inheritances, forbade cutting down hickory or pecan trees to get the nuts, punished gaming and disturbing public worship or other lawful gatherings. The whipping laws provided that the lashes should be "well laid on" and this was done in every case.

In later years they had laws that governed their own people and their own lands, even after United States

[204]

Courts were set up for trial of offenders not citizens, or of offenses against non-citizens. They had decorum in their courts, and enforced it. While Judge Absalom James was holding district court at Alikchi in the Choctaw Nation, in July, 1898, a Negro deputy sheriff from Towson County, east of Alikchi, walked into the court smoking a cigar, which was not permitted. Judge James ordered a fine of $2.50 for contempt of court. The Negro did not at once pay the fine, so when court ended for the day the judge ordered Sheriff Thomas Watson to put the Negro in jail and have him work out the fine.

The Negro said there were not enough men in Alikchi to put him in jail, and showed resistance, but he was overcome and pretty badly battered before he decided to give up and pay the fine. He made threats he would kill the deputies who arrested him, but did nothing toward carrying out the threat and returned to his own bailiwick.

There were laws against any person claiming to be a witch, or anyone charging another with being a witch, the punishment set at 60 lashes on the bare back. If anyone should kill another charged with being a witch the punishment was death.

Solomon Hotema killed three persons he said were witches, but he was not answerable to Indian laws because it was in 1899, when the Indian laws, except for misdemeanors, had been abrogated and the Federal Courts had jurisdiction. Hotema was a full-blood Choctaw who when a youth had attended Spencer Academy, a boarding school established by the Choctaw government in 1842. Hotema enrolled in 1870 and at the end of the time allowed each student he was one of several young Choctaws sent to Roanoke College, in Salem, Virginia, where he spent three years, returning home in 1880 before graduating. He was an able man, served as district attorney, county judge, representative in the tribal council and an interpreter, speaking both Choctaw and English fluently.

[205]

Hotema was a member of the Presbyterian Church, and assisted the Reverend J. P. Gibbons, a mission preacher and teacher at Goodwater, acting as interpreter until Mr. Gibbons learned Choctaw. Hotema became a licensed minister. He owned his home at Goodland and offered to give it to Mr. Gibbons if the latter would come and take charge of the Goodland mission school and orphan home. Mr. Gibbons accepted, and Hotema built for himself a house at Cold Spring, four miles west of Goodland orphanage. He was a good pulpit speaker and well liked as a minister.

Despite his education and ministerial experience, Hotema apparently never did rid himself of the ancient Indian superstition about witches. One day in April, 1899, he took his shot gun and in deliberate succession shot and killed Viney Coleman, Lucy Greenwood and Amos Harris. He said a medicine man had named the three as witches, so he killed them.

There are two stories of the origin of Hotema's determination to kill witches. Peter J. Hudson, himself an educated Choctaw, who knew Hotema well, said there had been a number of deaths from an obscure disease among members of Hotema's congregation, and the pastor was told by his friend, the "medicine man," that witches were killing the people. Judge T. C. Humphrey, who defended Hotema in his first two trials, and got an acquittal on the plea of insanity, said his client told him he killed the witches because he was not getting the expected and desired response to his preaching, and that witches were the cause of the trouble. Both stories agree that the medicine man told Hotema who were the witches, and both stories may be true. He may have had both causes for his act.

The trials were held before Judge David E. Bryant in Paris, Texas, in 1900, and Hotema was acquitted by juries for two of the killings on his plea of insanity. Later he was examined and pronounced sane and was arraigned for the

[206]

third killing. A witness was asked by one of the attorneys for Hotema as to his acquaintance, hoping to get testimony to show insanity in this trial also. After asking the usual questions the attorney asked, "Would you say he was sane or insane?" Aiming expertly at a cuspidor, and with great dignity, the witness replied, "Well, from the irrationality of his conduct, I would consider him sane."

Jake Hodges, a Paris lawyer, one of the most successful defenders at the bar in Paris, read to the jury Exodus 22:18, "Thou shalt not suffer a witch to live," and argued that Hotema had been obeying the Divine injunction, but the jury found him guilty of murder and he was sentenced to be hanged.

T. C. Humphrey, an eminent lawyer in Indian Territory, was principal counsel for Hotema. He went to Washington and induced President McKinley to commute the sentence to life imprisonment in the penitentiary. Hotema was taken to the penitentiary in Atlanta, Georgia, where he died in 1907. Mr. Humphrey, who later was appointed and served as a Federal Judge in Central District of Oklahoma, continued efforts for Hotema and appealed, though in vain, to President Theodore Roosevelt for a pardon.

In 1894 a Negro was elected to the Choctaw Council from Kiamichi County, which included part of what is the modern Choctaw County, and went to Tushkahoma and presented credentials but was refused a seat by the Council. The treaty the Choctaws made with the Federal Government, after the fall of the Southern Confederacy in 1865, had provided that Negro citizens, by adoption, marriage or otherwise, should have the same rights as the Choctaws, but the Council evidently did not understand this to include holding office, and exercised its right to determine the qualifications of its own members.

After Federal Courts were established in Indian Territory the Indian tribes were allowed to have some authority. One of the rules of the Interior Department gave the

Indians power to collect grazing fees from owners of cattle using the lands for their herds, and to require non-citizens to have a permit and pay a fee to do business in the Nation. In 1905 two white men at Atoka were arrested by Indian Policeman E. M. Wilson and their deportation from the Nation was ordered by the Indian Agent and Superintendent of Indian Affairs. The men had not paid permit fees and were alleged to be holding land contrary to law. The men appealed to the Federal Court, asserting they owned property in the town of Atoka.

Judge T. C. Humphrey heard the case and found title to the land in Atoka was obtained after the men were arrested; that the purchase was a subterfuge; and finally that he had no jurisdiction because the matter was one for the Interior Department. The Judge refused the injunction and the policeman took the two men and put them across Red River into Texas. If they returned the penalty was $1,000 each, so they stayed out of the Choctaw Nation.

The grazing fee for non-citizens' cattle was 20 cents per head annually. If not paid the cattle could be seized and one dollar a head had to be paid to regain possession of them. The money from these tribal permits and fines was put into the tribal funds and administered by the Indian Agent.

CIVIL GOVERNMENT

"The only orthodox object of the institution of government is to secure the greatest degree of happiness possible to the general mass of those associated under it."   *—Thomas Jefferson*

THE SOUTHERN VALLEY

Red River County . . . . *Clarksville*
Fannin County . *Bonham, Honey Grove*
Lamar County . . *Paris, Arthur City*
Bowie County . . *Boston, Texarkana*
Grayson County . . *Sherman, Denison*

THE NORTHERN VALLEY

McCurtain County . . . . . *Idabel*
Choctaw County . . . . . . *Hugo*
Bryan County . . . . . . *Durant*

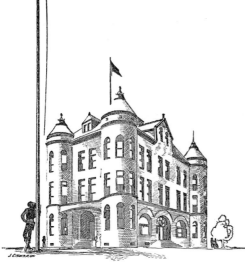

Red River County

WHEN THE DELEGATES from the Valley went to the Convention that adopted the Texas Declaration of Independence they were registered as being from "Pecan Point and vicinity" and it was after the victory at San Jacinto that the area was called Red River County.

It was realized by the Congress that the county was far too large to continue as a political division of the Republic, and the western half, into which a number of colonists had gone the previous year, was made Fannin County. Three years later the county was again divided by creation of Lamar and Bowie Counties, but Red River County, despite its reduction in area, continued to be the most thickly settled county in the Valley.

Clarksville was the oldest permanent settlement in the county, except Jonesboro, on Red River, which was still used by Miller County, Arkansas, as its county seat, and was so used until the boundary between Texas and United States was definitely known by survey. James Clark, a Tennesseean who had come to Miller County, Arkansas, and lived for a time in Jonesboro, had traded with Henry Stout for some land on which the City of Clarksville now stands. Clark moved to this land in 1835 and was preparing to build his house when Isaac Smathers and his family came, expecting to go further into Texas. Clark persuaded Smathers to stop, gave him a piece of land, and helped build a house. Other immigrants came, and the settlement grew.

Court was held at LaGrange, a settlement northeast of Clark's settlement, and LaGrange was incorporated by an act of the Congress in November, 1837. Less than a month later, the same session of the Congress incorporated Clarksville. Robert Hamilton was elected chief justice for the

[211]

county and was to hold election for other county officers and appoint commissioners to nominate a site for the county seat. This was done and the voters chose Clarksville. A log court house was built in the public square, which was the center of the land Clark had given for the county seat.

Clarksville soon became an educational center, and to that was attributed much of its growth. Less than four years after it was made the county seat, the Reverend J. W. P. McKenzie opened his school a few miles from the town. In the town within a short time, were the Female Seminary, conducted by Mrs. Weatherred and her son-in-law, the Reverend James Graham, who had come from Pennsylvania; the Female Institute, managed by Mrs. Eliza Todd; and the Clarksville Classical, Mathematical and Mercantile Academy, conducted by the Reverend John Anderson and Alexander T. Russell. All took boarding pupils, one advertising to give this service, including washing, candles and fuel, for $8 per month.

About the same time Charles DeMorse came to Clarksville and began publication of the *Northern Standard,* a journal that for years was influential in shaping Texas thought and policies. It also did much toward making Clarksville a desirable place in which to live and rear a family, and the town continued to grow.

A number of men who remained in Red River County were of more than ordinary influence. Travis Wright, oldest living son of Claiborne Wright, remained at Kiamichi and operated a store and a line of boats on Red River. James Latimer and his sons, one of whom, Albert, was a signer of the Declaration, congressman and legislator, and served briefly as State Comptroller and later as a chief justice of Texas Supreme Court. Henry Latimer, another son, educated at Princeton, lawyer and Senator in the Texas Legislature. James Titus, Senator of the Republic, came to Texas in 1832. He was employed by the Federal Government to aid in removing the Indians to their Ter-

[*212*]

ritory and settled permanently near Clarksville in 1839, opened a plantation and established the first post office at Clarksville. The Reverend Samuel Corley who came in 1840 and preached over a great part of the Valley, was pastor of the Presbyterian Church which had been consolidated with the Shiloh congregation which was formed in 1833. When the war with Mexico came, Mr. Corley and one of his sons went to the front, and he resumed preaching when that affair ended. Later he was a chaplain in a Confederate regiment when the war between the sections began, but asked for and was given a commission as captain of cavalry. Promoted to be a major he died in September, 1863, of wounds suffered at the battle of Bayou Fourche, near Little Rock, Arkansas, just after his regiment had captured a Federal battery.

A resident of Red River County for a time who attained some notoriety was Albert Fall. He was a Kentuckian who came to Red River County about 1880, farmed for a time, then went into real estate as an agent, with Joseph Brittain. Their advertisement in the *Clarksville Standard,* 1883, said they were "Real estate and land agents. Lands bought, abstracts procured, surveys made, taxes paid. All business attended to promptly."

About the same time Fall went to Tennessee and there married Miss Emma Morgan, who was reared in Clarksville, daughter of Simpson Morgan who died while a Texas representative in the Confederate Congress. Presently Fall went to New Mexico, then a Territory, and was a member of the convention that wrote the Constitution for the State which was admitted to the Union in 1912, and Fall was elected one of its senators. He was made Secretary of the Interior under President Harding and in 1922 signed the lease of the Teapot Dome oil district to the Sinclair interests, and the Elk Hills oil reserve to E. C. Doheny. Federal investigation led to indictments. Sinclair and Doheny were acquitted, but Fall was convicted of accepting from Doheny $100,000, and served some time in prison.

Clarksville for years was a hotbed of politics, partly by reason of DeMorse and his newspaper, and because it was the home of many men who were prominent in affairs of the State. DeMorse had been rather neutral in national politics, but when a newspaper was established in Clarksville, which announced its devotion to the cause of the Whig Party, in 1847, DeMorse began his stout advocacy of the Democratic Party and continued it, though the new paper had a short life. He supported the nomination of Cass for president by the split Democratic Convention in Baltimore, in 1848, and printed a call for a mass meeting and barbecue in Clarksville, July 22, 1848, to express ratification of the nomination. The Standard predicted defeat of the Whigs and Zachary Taylor, their candidate, but this did not come to pass. The rally and barbecue were held with much enthusiasm and fiery speeches, and was only one of many such gatherings in the county from time to time.

Red River County has always been primarily an agricultural area, though the timber supplied and still supplies material for some saw mills. Most of the early-day houses within a hundred miles of Clarksville were built of lumber sawed in Red River County, after building houses of logs was discontinued. For years Red River County was famed for its long-staple cotton, which was marketed in Clarksville and brought double or more what the ordinary staple sold for, but its production has almost ceased in recent years.

Fannin County

FANNIN COUNTY was so large that in 1844, five years after it was created, the Congress of Texas made two court districts. Everything west of a line drawn south from the mouth of Choctaw Bayou at Red River went to court at the house of Seamon Bradley. All east of the line went to

[214]

court in Bonham, which had been selected as county seat.

Fannin's first court house was built at Warren, on Red River, and court was held there until Bonham, originally called Bois d'arc, was chosen. Bailey Inglish had built his block house about a mile east of the Bois d'arc settlement, and a temporary court house was built in Bonham. The county was reduced in size in 1846, by creation of Grayson, Hunt and Collin counties. The population had increased and the need for a larger and better court house was felt. This was to be of brick and was begun in 1849. Dr. Edward Smith, an Englishman looking over the Valley for a location for a proposed colony, said he saw a specimen of the brick, which was of very bad quality, apparently having too much sand mixed with the clay.

Dr. Smith, the English traveler, told something of Bonham. He said, "Stores and trades of various kinds are established, and a bi-weekly newspaper is published which deserves to be the organ of a larger populated locality. The editor is foremost to give information to adventuring parties going to California by this route.

"The Indians are peaceable, many cultivating the land and carrying on civilized occupations in their Territory, but the cheap whisky from Cincinnati distilleries is introduced by traders and has a most pernicious tendency. One of these traders was in the boat with us from Cincinnati to Jefferson, bringing with him enough whisky to load two wagons, to be sold to Indians.

"In Bonham we saw some of the finest horses in America, many $16\frac{1}{2}$ hands, well proportioned and valued at $100. They have been introduced from the old states and are now bred on the prairies."

During Reconstruction, Captain J. E. Caraway, who had been an officer in the Confederate Army, was registrar of voters in northern Fannin County. He started one day with his family to visit in the southern part of Texas, reaching Bonham about night. He saw Yankee soldiers in the

[*215*]

town and learned that Judge Hardin Hart had ended a session of court. Judge Hart was a son of John Hart, a noted pioneer, and was opposed to secession. He was appointed district judge by the military government and therefore was not liked by some of the unreconstructed Rebels.

Next morning Caraway left Bonham and five miles south of town met a squad of Yankee cavalry. He gave them the road, and when the rear horsemen reached him he asked why they were hurrying. He was told that Judge Hart and Judge Gray, a lawyer, had been shot from ambush down the road and they were going to Bonham for reinforcements. Presently they returned from Bonham with more soldiers and some citizens, and going down the road found a dead horse but no dead men. Later they learned that Judge Gray had not been wounded from ambush but Judge Hart's left arm was broken and had to be amputated. Hart continued on the bench after the State was returned to its own government several years later.

Bois d'arc Bayou was sometimes not fordable, and bridges were built over it from time to time, but were washed out by floods. In 1871 the Legislature granted a charter to Alexander Inglish and associates to build a bridge east of Bonham, that would stand floods, and authority to charge tolls. This bridge lasted a long time. An earlier bridge had been built by Bailey Inglish, the pioneer who built the block house near where Bonham was later established, and he also collected tolls.

After Bailey Inglish died his estate was divided and that part that included the bridge fell to his daughter, Mrs. Thomas Cowart. Two of her sons tended the bridge and collected tolls. The story is told that one day while Charley Cowart was on duty a young man came to cross the bridge. He was rather smart in his talk, and Charley offered to bet that he could cut the fellow's hat to pieces and put it together again. The smart youngster was finally persuaded to bet five cents against the bridge fare of a dime. Cowart cut the hat to pieces, and after apparently trying to put it together again admitted he could not do so and that he had lost his bet, which allowed the hatless youth to cross the bridge without paying money.

Fannin county has been visited by tornadoes more than once. The most destructive was one night in May, 1880, when the town of Savoy, in the western edge of the county, was destroyed by a twister that killed thirteen people and several died from injuries. Almost every building in the town was destroyed.

There have been tragedies in Fannin County as well as in all other counties in the Valley. One of the most famous was concerning the "Dyer boys" who were two characters who have become almost legendary. Sheriff Ragsdale and his deputy, Buchanan, went to the home of the Dyers near Edhube, a village, to arrest them for one of their numerous offenses. The officers were told by the mother that her sons were not at home. Some horses were on the place and the officers began looking for the men. Ragsdale looked through a crack in the smokehouse and saw the men hiding inside, but before he could start to the door to get them he was shot in the head through the crack in the house. The Dyers came out and killed Buchanan and left the place.

Some time afterwards they were caught by a posse of citizens and put in jail in Bonham. A hanging party was arranged and so quietly they acted that the people living near where the Dyers were hung to a bois d'arc tree were surprised next morning to see the bodies swinging from a limb. The tree was afterwards sawed into small blocks from which were made cuff buttons and other curios.

Some Indians came over to the Bryant plantation on Red River in Fannin County in 1872 to pick cotton. Two of them lived in a tent, got drunk, and Alfred killed Moses. He went to the house, called Mr. Bryant and said, "Bryant,

I died Moses." The dead Indian was buried and Alfred was advised to leave before the brothers of Moses came and killed him. Alfred declined to go, and one night as he stood by the fire outside his tent he was shot and that was the last of it.

In December, 1889, a company was billed to play "Uncle Tom's Cabin," in the opera house over one of the stores on the Bonham public square. A day or two before the performance, Jefferson Davis, only president of the defeated Confederacy, passed away. Some Bonham citizens asked the opera house manager to cancel the performance, but he said he could not do it. The night of the performance the street in front was packed with men and boys with tin pans, whistles, giant firecrackers, horns, anything that would make a noise. The curtain rose with six paying customers in the house but by the time the first act began half a dozen men with guns entered. They did not shoot the actors, but they did shoot out some lights and the crowd outside began its cacophony that brought the show to an end. The actors scattered without waiting to remove the makeup. Little Eva and the bloodhounds wandered off and got back to the hotel late. Uncle Tom and Simon Legree and Topsy sought the open air. No one was injured physically, but the company left Bonham wiser than when they arrived. Bonham would stand some things, but not a "Tom" show while the body of Jefferson Davis lay in state awaiting the reverent burial that the South gave him.

Honey Grove, a small city now, on the east edge of Fannin County, was a rival of Bonhan for a time and was once designated to be a county seat for a county to be named Webster County, whether in honor of Noah or Daniel was not stated. The radical constitutional convention of 1868-69, while Texas was in the grip of the Federal military overlords, made a "Declaration" that seven miles should be taken from Lamar County and ten

[*218*]

miles from Fannin County, and be formed into a county to be named Webster, with Honey Grove as the county seat. The organization was never made, and presently the declaration was forgotten. In the 'eighties of the last century, when the Santa Fe Rail Road was coming from the south, Honey Grove made a bid for it, but got only a tap from Ladonia, the main line coming on to Paris for a junction with the Frisco. Honey Grove in those days had the nickname of "The Maude S. of Fannin County," so fast was the town growing and so energetic were the people in getting civic improvements.

Both Bonham and Honey Grove have grown since those early days, and are two of the best small cities in the Valley, with churches and schools of the best type and homes of people who are proud of their forefathers who brought order out of confusion during a hundred years.

Lamar County

Lamar County's first permanent home builder was John Emberson, and his coming to Texas was due not to an itching foot but to a "hot foot" in this wise: John was born in Virginia in 1798 and was taken by his parents to Kentucky where he attended backwoods school. One morning there came to the school a gangling youth, who was wearing shoes too large for him and the ankles gaped. Sitting by the log fire in the school house, John picked up a hot coal and dropped it in the newcomer's shoe. There was a fight and the teacher essayed to whip John, as was proper, but John objected to being whipped and left. When he reached home and had to tell his father why he was not in school the father gave what the teacher had not been able to give, so John left home.

Meeting some soldiers bound for New Orleans to fight with Andrew Jackson against the British, he joined them and was one of the youths behind the cotton bale breastworks. In the Army John became acquainted with Allen

[219]

Carter, a married man who lived in Arkansas, then a part of Missouri Territory, and John was invited to go home with Carter. The next Winter, 1815-16, they trapped along Red River as far west as Lamar County of today. After going back to Arkansas John married one of Carter's daughters, and lived in the Pecan Point and Clear Creek settlements.

When settlers in that area were being removed so Indians could have their land, John Emberson remembered the places where he had trapped. He and his family went west and settled in what is now Lamar County, with his wife and their sons, Eldridge and Elijah, and their daughter, Eliza. They made their home near Red River in 1824, and there another son was born and named John.

By 1836 more settlers had come in and were coming in increasing numbers. John A. Rutherford, who was Lamar's first chief justice, was west of Emberson. Sam Fulton had established his trading post on the river east of Emberson. Lawrence Tinnin was still further down the river. Matt Click had come and went out on the prairie south of where now is Paris. Leven Moore had come with his brothers-in-law and stopped a few miles east of the site of Paris, and Claiborne Chisum had built his house where now is a part of Paris, with others settling in various localities.

It was getting too crowded along the river for Emberson, so he moved to land he had been given on the prairie several miles from the river and farmed. A few years later he again became "crowded" and this time moved to the far west, where he had acquired a large tract in Grayson County that lapped over into Denton and Collin Counties, where he spent the remainder of his life.

Claiborne Chisum came in 1836 and bought land from Asa Jarman who had located a headright almost in the middle of what was to be Lamar County. A few years later his brother-in-law, Epps Gibbons, came with his family

[220]

and built his home a mile from the log court house that was then built in the middle of the public square. The log house was built by Major George W. Stell, who later was appointed by the Congress to survey and superintend cutting timber and building bridges on the Central National Road of the Republic, from near the three forks of the Trinity to the mouth of the Kiamichi—a road that came through the Paris public square. Major Stell had taken the contract to build the log court house by a given date, provided it did not interfere with the gathering of his crop. He, like many others, was a farmer, growing his own grain and other products.

Lamar was able to build a brick house by 1846 and the contract was taken by Claiborne Chisum and Epps Gibbons. The latter made the brick near his home and his two sons, Edward and John Gibbons, and two of Chisum's sons, John and James, carried the brick and mortar, for Z. M. Paul who laid the brick. Five years later John Chisum was elected Lamar County Clerk, but left before his term was ended and began ranching in Denton County, going eventually to New Mexico, where two of his brothers joined him in cattle raising. The Gibbons sons, John and Ed, later were mayors of Paris.

Claiborne Wright and his oldest son, William, both had died before Texas independence, and Travis and George Wright, younger sons, lived in Jonesboro. While George was in South Texas in 1836, a lieutenant in a company that had gone from Red River to help Sam Houston (but arrived too late to get in the battle of San Jacinto) he was elected a member of the First Texas Congress and at the same time his brother, Travis, was a member of the Arkansas Constitutional Convention in Little Rock. Arkansas still claimed what later proved to be a part of Texas.

George Wright tired of the river where there was much illness. He rode to the divide between Red and Sulphur Rivers, sold his plantation at Kiamichi to his brother

[221]

Travis, and bought a thousand acres of land from Larkin Rattan, adjoining Chisum's land, in 1839, built a store and a home and the next year was instrumental in getting the Congress to divide Red River County, leaving him in the center of Lamar County. He gave the county fifty acres of his land for a county seat, with his store on a lot facing the public square of Paris, which he had named his settlement.

Paris became incorporated and grew slowly but steadily, presently becoming more populous than either Clarksville, Bonham or Sherman. The county government functioned as did those of the other counties, with courts being held, some roads being cut through timber and drained after a fashion, paupers were cared for, churches and schools were built, merchants and professional men came and life settled down on a fairly even level.

Incidents of government in Lamar were like those in the other counties in many respects, and were different from today. As example: people unable to support themselves were by the county commissioners declared to be paupers. There was no poor house and the paupers were sold to the lowest bidder. That is, the sheriff would hold sales at intervals, and the person who made the lowest bid to care for and feed and clothe a pauper was awarded the one then at auction. At one sale the sheriff failed to get a bid for a man who was an epileptic, and later the justice in whose precinct the man lived reported he had found a man who would take care of this epileptic for $250 a year. In 1876 there was an order by the commissioners that "Mrs. Cardwell, a pauper, be removed from the roll, she having married during the past month." Cupid worked then as well as now and in as various ways. Presently the commissioners established a poor farm and maintained it until Social Security came to replace it.

Jails were none too strong, apparently, and prisoners were ironed in some cases if they were being held for serious crimes. Irons were welded on their ankles, and in 1857 a Paris blacksmith was ordered to be paid $33 for "ironing and unironing" certain prisoners. Medical attention to prisoners was also let by bids, the doctor bidding the lowest for the service being engaged by the year. The commissioners refused to approve a bill for a pint of whisky for the use of a prisoner, but did allow a monthly sum to buy morphine for an addict who lived with his brother-in-law and the record said, "Was kept alive by use of morphine."

Some odd things appear in probate records. Joshua Bowerman operated a distillery in the early 'forties, and when he died claims against his estate included a note which read: "Due Robert Campbell, for value received of him for services rendered to this date, eleven dollars, 42 cents, to be paid in whisky at $1 per gallon—11½ gallons," Robert had apparently never gotten the whisky.

Lamar County voted against secession from the Union and was joined by Fannin and Grayson Counties. Red River and Bowie Counties favored secession. Lamar County had three delegates—George W. Wright and Lemuel H. Williams, merchants, and William H. Johnson, a prominent lawyer—to the convention that adopted the ordinance of secession. They and four other men from various parts of the State, cast the seven votes against the ordinance, which was overwhelmingly adopted.

The war brought suffering and deprivations to the people of the Valley, though no battles were fought on its soil. With most able-bodied men in the Army, farms were uncultivated or were partly cultivated, salt and medicines became scarce as the years passed. The counties had to provide for the families that had no adult members left, and the currency issued by the Confederate Government, and then by many of the counties, became increasingly depreciated. By 1863 some people refused to accept the paper money for debts, and a memorial was addressed to

[223]

the Legislature by nearly a hundred Lamar County citizens, asking that an act be passed, providing that when payment of a debt tendered in Confederate currency was refused, interest on the debt would cease from that time.

In the early 'fifties three brothers and their families came from England—Isaac, William and Frederick Parr—and settled on the high prairie several miles north of Paris. They bought 150 acres of land for $150, which they added to from time to time until they owned hundreds of acres and some lots or acreage in the corporate limits of Paris. They built a cotton gin and a mill for grinding wheat and corn, and became prosperous people, but they did not seek naturalization, and when the war between the sections began they raised the Union Jack over their mill to indicate they were neither Federal nor Confederate, and neither had nor wanted to have anything to do with the war.

In 1864, when the war was drawing to its end, Isaac Parr contracted with the Lamar County police court (now called the County Court) to supply 130 bushels of corn meal for the indigent families, at $9 per bushel, 50 bushels to be delivered in October and the balance during the next two months. Mr. Parr was paid, of course, with Confederate money, and unless he used it within six months it was just so much paper. The Parrs' descendants still live on the high prairie and are among the good citizens of the Valley.

It took the Valley only a few years to recover from the loss caused by the war. Farms were cultivated, houses built, county fairs began to be held, schools reopened, and the daily lives of the people went on much as before the conflict. The people had gone to work, and without help from the government, either State or National, they made it.

Paris has twice been visited by fires that each time destoryed a large part of the business district, the second

[224]

blaze taking hundreds of homes as well as stores, churches, schools and public buildings. Other towns and cities in the Valley have had fires but none that caused such great losses as those that swept Paris.

The first, on August 31, 1877, was started in a saloon on the south side of the public square by a young man, Taylor Pounds, who was angry because his step-father, Andy Myers, who owned the saloon refused to give him money. Pounds poured coal oil on the floor of a rear room in the wooden building and lighted it with a match. The fire swept the buildings off a dozen blocks, including three sides of the public square. Pounds was caught next day, hiding in the high weeds of a vacant lot on the edge of town, and after cool headed citizens had prevented his lynching, which some losers insisted should be his punishment, he was tried in Delta County on a change of venue, and given a term in the penitentiary.

The second fire, far more destructive, occurred March 21-22, 1916. It started from unknown cause in a small storage house in the southwestern edge of the city. Fanned by a strong wind, and finding dry grass in yards, and dry shingle roofs on residences, it spread rapidly, and in an hour was out of control. As the fire driven by a southwest wind went north, it spread to the northeast, the west line being nearly straight.

Firemen and apparatus came from Hugo, Oklahoma, from Bonham and Honey Grove, and soon after midnight of the 21st a big pump and men from Dallas came on a Santa Fe special train, in time to stop the eastern spread of the blaze, which had begun at 5:30 in the afternoon and was finally stopped about 4 o'clock the morning of the 22d. Nearly every building on 270 acres was destroyed. Losses were estimated at $8 million, with insurance of about $4½ million. The city was rebuilt within a year, even better than before.

The coming of two railroads to Paris in 1887 brought

[225]

an increase in population and business. One of them, the St. Louis & San Francisco from the north, caused the founding of a town on Red River that had hope of becoming a second Denison, such as the Katy Railroad created north of Sherman. The town was named Arthur City, and it might have fulfilled the dream of its founders but for the fact that Paris did not make the mistake of not providing the bonus and right-of-way from the river that was asked by the railroad. While the railroad and its bridge across the river were being built, Arthur City was a sizeable village, somewhat rough at times, but eventually its residents, or many of them, moved away, and left it a small country town.

There was a saloon in Arthur City when the railroad was being built, saloons being legal in Lamar County at the time. One day two men came from across the river and decided they wanted a drink but did not want to get off their horses. When one started to ride into the saloon the youth in charge, while the owner had come to Paris on business, asked them to dismount, but they refused and one rode in and was met by the youth who swung a large and heavy club that knocked the fellow off his horse. The other man got off his horse outside and went in to help his brother, and the two were about to get the best of the young man when a man who was his friend came in and took a hand, with the result that the two wouldbe horseback drinkers were thrown out without getting their whisky.

At another time the same two men came over at night and rode into a dance hall, disturbing the men and women who were on the floor. They were overpowered and carried out and thrown into Red River, after which the dance was resumed. The men swam out but did not return to the dance.

In the 'nineties of the last century a house boat was tied up on Red River not far from Arthur City. Three men were on board and it became known that they were not

[226]

averse to gambling and that whisky could be had of them if one made the right approach and had enough money. They offered fish for sale occasionally, but this was apparently a blind for their real occupation. One day a man hunting his horses on the north side of the river saw the boat and hailed it, thinking the men might have seen his horses getting water at the river. Getting no reply he went nearer and through a window saw three men and a boy laying on the floor of the cabin. He started to go on board but a fierce dog challenged him and he backed off, went to Arthur City and asked the railroad telegraph operator to notify United States Marshal J. Shelby Williams in Paris.

Marshal Williams went to the place, with Joe Everidge, a special deputy who lived at Grant, not far from the river in the Territory. They coaxed the dog and got it tied, and found four bodies in the cabin. The men were never identified, but the boy was Paul Applegate 14 years old, son of a Paris family, who had run away from home and had evidently been allowed on board by the men.

Everidge presently got evidence that caused arrest of two Negro men in the Territory. One of them, a mulatto, John Willis, confessed, but the other, Bill Hickman, a short, black Negro, made no confession nor denial. The Negroes had been to a festival and traded some articles. When arrested they still had in their possession articles that were known to have been on the boat. When Deputy Everidge discovered this the confession was made and later substantiated by other evidence.

The confession said the two had gone on the boat, gambled with the men and lost. A few days later they returned, determined to get back their money, but again they lost. They then asked permission to sleep on the boat, as it was near night. They stayed awake, and when the men and boy were asleep the Negroes took axes and crushed the heads of the three men. The boy waked and was shot. The

[227]

Negroes then took all the money they could find, and the articles that led to their arrest, and left. They were tried in Federal Court before Judge David E. Bryant and hanged. Hickman died happy, humming a hymn under his black cap, but Willis was silent.

Many years before Arthur City was founded, a Paris citizen had a boat on Red River from which he sold whisky legally. The south bank of the river was the boundary, so he was not in Texas. He had a Federal license to sell liquor, and a marine license for his boat, because the river was still considered navigable as it had been years before. He said if Federal officers talked of arresting him he showed his licenses, whereupon they would take a drink he offered them and let him alone. When he was arrested by Texas officers for selling without a license from Texas he was acquitted, because no part of the river was in Texas. When enforcement of the "No whisky" in Indian Territory law began, he quit, but he said he had made considerable money.

Bowie County

BOWIE COUNTY and Lamar County are twins, both having been created by one bill of the Texas Congress, approved by Vice President David G. Burnett, December 17, 1840. Bowie County is the only county in the Valley named for a hero of the Alamo. It was the home of men who helped make the Valley a good place in which to build a home and rear a family, and who gave service to the Republic and the State from the beginning.

Some of these men were citizens of Red River County before it was divided, and became and remained citizens of Bowie County. Richard Ellis, one of the delegates from Red River district to the Convention that adopted the Declaration and the Constitution, was familiar with such proceedings. A Virginian who practiced law in his native

[228]

state, he moved to Alabama and was a member of that state's Constitutional Convention and then a Circuit Judge. Returning to Virginia he was made an Associate Justice of the Virginia Supreme Court, but after three years on the bench he came to Texas and settled near Red River in what became Bowie County. He was a Senator in the first four Texas Congresses, then retired to his home where he died on December 20, 1846. Exactly three years after his death, the Texas Legislature created Ellis County, named in his honor.

Collin McKinney came from Tennessee to Texas in 1824, settling with his family near present-day Texarkana. Native of New Jersey he had lived in Kentucky and Tennessee before coming to Texas. He was a signer of the Declaration and served in three sessions of the Texas Congress. A professional surveyor, he is said to be responsible for the regular shape and size of the newer-created Texas counties. A Texas Legislature chose his first name for a county name and his family name for its county seat.

Matthias Ward was a Georgian who came to what became Bowie County in 1836. He engaged in trading, though he had taught school and studied law. He was a Representative in the Seventh and Eighth Texas Congresses and active in Texas Masonic work. After annexation he served one term in the State Senate. In 1858 he was appointed by Governor Runnels to be United States Senator to succeed J. P. Henderson who had died. When Texas seceded the seats of Matt Ward and John Hemphill were declared vacant. Ward died two years later.

Perhaps the most famous of the Red River men who became citizens of Bowie County was Edward H. Tarrant. Born in North Carolina he fought under Andrew Jackson in Indian campaigns and at the battle of New Orleans, came to Texas in 1835 and after the Revolution became a Ranger and Indian fighter, resigning from the Congress to resume command on the frontier. He represented Bowie County in the Annexation Convention, then moved to Central Texas and died some years later.

Bowie County inherited from Red River County the College of DeKalb. It had been chartered by the Congress in 1839, and was given about 18,000 acres of land which could be sold or leased and the money used for the College. The charter required the College must be "conducted for students of all religious denominations" and was to make "paramount the promotion of learning, morality and virtue." It was given jurisdiction over all land within half a mile of the College to suppress nuisances and levy fines not less than $25 nor more than $100 on sellers of spirituous liquors within that territory, which were "to be collected for the College by the sheriff of Red River County."

When the Legislature created Bowie County it provided that court was to be held at DeKalb until the citizens selected a county seat. The village of Boston, near the center of the county was chosen and a court house was built there. When the Transcontinental Rail Road was built it ran several miles north of Boston, whereupon most of the businesses and people of the town picked up and started a town at the railroad, calling it New Boston. The vote of the people had said the court house should be in the geographical center of the county, and when it was proposed to move the county seat to the railroad that requirement was cited. A careful survey was made and it was found that Boston was south of the center, but that the actual center was something more than a mile south of the railroad. So a court house was built on the prairie, in sight of New Boston, and there the county seat remains, despite some attempts of Texarkana to have it moved to that city, the voters refusing to sanction the change.

Old Boston, as the original settlement came to be called, was the principal settlement between Jefferson and Clarksville, and but for removal of the court house would proba-

[230]

bly have been a considerable town today. When the first court house was wrecked the foundation was left, and years afterwards a school house was built on the foundation, which was still substantial.

Bowie County knew how to play practical politics, even though it might not always be exactly as the law provided. In the 'nineties of the last century Dave Culberson, who had represented the First Congressional District for near twenty years, was opposed in the general election by J. H. Davis of Sulphur Springs. Davis, commonly known as "Methodist Jim" and later as "Cyclone" was at that particular time a Populist leader and spell-binder. It was generally understood that Davis got the most votes but the returns showed Culberson had a small majority and it was said that what was known as the Shaw voting box in Bowie County was responsible for the votes that elected Culberson. The voting box was on a plantation owned by Gus Shaw, a practical politician, whose Negro hands voted as they were told. One of Shaw's cronies told once that Gus said the hardest job he ever had was to think up 125 names and put them on the poll list, and deposit corresponding ballots, properly marked, in the ballot box.

The Shaw box never had to send corrections. It just waited making returns until the others had reported, and its returns were sent in to meet the need, if any. Colonel Sheb Williams, a Lamar County political leader, once sent word to Gus, asking "Why in hell don't you send in your returns?" Gus responded, "Why in hell don't you let me know how many are needed?" The Shaw box flourished before the days of the Terrell election law, and Gus was a Democrat of the old school.

Bowie County had for years a health resort south of De-Kalb, known as Dalby Springs, which supplied water that was almost red from the iron content. There was a hotel and cottages, and people from over North Texas came to spend part of the Summer and drink the water, which really had medicinal quality. The hotel was kept by J. W. Farrier, who owned the land on which the spring flowed, and besides the hotel he did considerable shipping of water.

Texarkana, another city that owes its birth to railroads, was laid out astride the Texas-Arkansas state line, in a pine forest. It was the beginning point of the Transcontinental and the terminus of the St. Louis, Iron Mountain and Southern, which had been begun as the Cairo and Fulton. There was a sale of town lots in December, 1873. One of the buyers was A. L. Ghio, an Italian who came to America when a youth. He had been in many cities and engaged in various businesses, but Texarkana held him. On his lot he built a box house and opened a liquor, tobacco and cigar business within a few weeks. He made money, invested it in real estate that increased in value as the town grew. Presently he owned several business houses and an "opera house" and was elected mayor, serving several terms, refusing re-election in 1886. When his life ended he was one of the wealthiest men in Texarkana.

There was a tragedy in Texarkana in July, 1882. The story was retold some years later by W. B. Weeks, an early-day newspaper man. The Paragon saloon was a frame building, as were most of the buildings in the town, then about eight years old. On the lot adjoining the Paragon A. L. Ghio was building a three-story brick business house. The walls had just been finished to where the roof would be put on. One night when the Paragon was well filled, dark clouds appeared, that brought rain and a strong wind. Soon after 8 o'clock a crash was heard and it was found that the brick walls of the Ghio house had collapsed and crushed the Paragon like an egg shell. Three men near the door were able to get out before the Paragon roof crashed. The oil lamps that lighted the saloon set fire to the ruins and people not already dead were cremated. One man pinned under the wreckage, but not killed, who saw the fire approaching him, called to the men trying to rescue some of the victims that they could not get to him in time. Then he shot himself. The number who lost their lives was never known, for no one knew how many or who were in the saloon, but several well-known citizens, including a bartender who had been an early-day mayor of the town, were among the dead. Ghio afterwards bought the Paragon lot and on it and his other lot built a two-story house, the second floor of which was his opera house, and which twenty years later was destroyed by fire.

Mr. Weeks recalled another tragedy in Texarkana, this one occurring in that part of the town lying in Arkansas. It was less than a year after the Paragon disaster. Judge Mitchell was holding district court in Texarkana, county seat of Miller County, and Charles Dixon was sheriff. One day Ed Johnson came into court. He was under indictment on a charge of gaming and was what was called a professional gambler. It was said that Dixon had made his living that way until he went into politics and was elected sheriff.

As Johnson walked down the aisle toward the judge's bench, Sheriff Dixon met him, drew his gun and fired. The bullet struck Johnson in the left eye, another struck him in the neck as he was falling and a third made a hole between his eyes as his body laid on the floor. Dixon walked to the judge's bench, laid down his gun and said he surrendered.

The judge told the clerk to enter an order on his minutes, suspending the sheriff from office, then swore the deputy clerk as sheriff, who arrested Dixon and took him to jail. Dixon made bond and insisted on early trial which was held a few days afterwards and he was acquitted. The defense was that Johnson had slandered Mrs. Dixon and that he shot Johnson the first time he saw him after being informed of the slander.

After acquittal Dixon resumed the office of sheriff but was defeated for re-election. There were rumors that there had been no slander but that the trouble rose over a gam-

[233]

bling house raid. Dixon went back to gambling and eleven years later was shot and killed on a Texarkana street, oddly enough by a man named Johnson, also a gambler though not related to the man Dixon had killed, and even more oddly Johnson claimed Dixon had slandered Johnson's wife. He was never tried nor even indicted, quit gambling and moved to another town.

Texarkana, like all new railroad junction and terminal towns in those days, and like the oil towns of later days, was a resort for some tough characters, but finally a fair degree of law and order prevailed, the town grew into a city—or two cities, for each side of the state line had and has separate governments—and became prosperous as a manufacturing center.

Grayson County

GRAYSON is the youngest of the Texas counties included in this Valley. It was created by taking part of Fannin County in 1846 and organized soon afterwards. While a court house was building, a court was held in the home of Bob Acheson, on Iron Ore Creek, by James G. Thompson, chief justice, and his associates Nicholas Maddox and William Lankford. James Randolph was sheriff.

The first court house was of logs, four miles west of the present site of Sherman. When completed there was a barbecue and one who attended described it afterwards. He said a log house about 20 feet square and a few rods of plowed ground composed the future metropolis. Under a brush arbor were tables of many things good to eat, all free. The refreshment stand was a rail fence built partly around a barrel of whisky with a tin cup set by it. After the feast there was a dance in the court house, music furnished by a Negro fiddler, who was relieved at intervals by another so the tired musician could refresh himself at the barrel.

Wood and good water were scarce around the court house and next year, when T. J. Shannon offered to donate land four miles east for a county seat, it was accepted, and another court house of logs was built on what is now the Sherman public square. Shannon was paid five dollars for moving the county property to the new site, and pending building the court house court was held under a big pecan tree at the southeast corner of the square and a small cabin housed the records.

A daughter of Shannon, then ten years old, was allowed to name the principal streets. She honored four Texas heroes by naming the streets Travis, Crockett, Houston and Lamar. She had seen buffalo and wild horses on the prairies and attended church when some of the people who came from a distance carried their guns, for Indians were still not far away.

By 1853 the log court house was too small and dilapidated for use and the commissioners advertised for bids to build one of brick, which was to be "paid for out of the revenue donated by the State of Texas to the various counties, to enable them to build Public Edifices, Etc." This house was built, replacing the log house and stood many years.

At the end of the Methodist conference year in 1847 the Reverend Mr. Brown, Presiding Elder Custer, and the Reverend Mr. Duncan, a missionary from the Indian Territory, held a camp meeting at Warren, a settlement on Red River, where had been the county seat of Fannin county when it was created. It had been a trading post established by Abel Warren in 1836, but abandoned by him when the trade with Indians proved not profitable. At this meeting, said the chronicler of the affair, was laid the foundation of Methodism in Grayson County.

Another trading post was established in the early days by Holland Coffee, who selected Preston Bend as his location. Coffee had been a member of a firm of traders in Fort Smith, and came to the frontier, believing it more advantageous to his business. He represented Fannin

[235]

County in the Third Congress of Texas. He had married Sophia Sutton Field in Washington County and they traveled horseback to his post, where they lived in a clapboard shanty surrounded by a stockade to keep out marauding Indians. Coffee was reputed to be able to speak seven Indian dialects, and he served as intermediary in ransoming children who had been stolen by Indians when they ravaged the scattered settlements. Some years after his marriage, when he became prosperous, he built a home for himself and wife which he called Glen Eden, and lived there until 1846, when a merchant at Fort Washita, in the Indian Territory, had a quarrel with him and Coffee was fatally stabbed. The affair occurred at Coffee's home but the grand jury found no indictment, the testimony indicating it was a case of self defense.

Most of the Holland Coffee home site is under the water of Lake Texoma, formed by the dam in Red River near Denison. Judge Randolph Bryant, who owned the property had the house taken down with the purpose of rebuilding it on higher ground.

May 15, 1896, Sherman was struck by a tornado. There were 65 persons listed as killed and 58 others injured seriously enough to be hospitalized. Many homes were wrecked, and an iron bridge on Houston street was wrenched apart and left a mass of twisted metal. The tornado covered a path more than twenty miles long, but its principal force was in Sherman.

The California Overland Mail Route passed through Grayson County, with a station at Sherman. Henry Bates, superintendent of the line from Red River to Fort Chadbourne (north of present-day San Angelo), announced in the Sherman Patriot in July, 1858, that the route was from Memphis across Arkansas and Indian Territory to the Colbert Ferry, where Red River was crossed, then on the county road to Sherman and west on the county road to Cooke County line. Another station was at the home of

[236]

John R. Dearmond. The company proposed to carry mail and passengers and to make the journey from Memphis to San Francisco in 25 days. Relay stations were being established 12 miles apart, and the first passengers and mails were to be started on August 15, 1858.

One of the most colorful towns in the Valley then, which yet lacks a lot of being drab and commonplace, as witness the celebration in September, 1947, of its seventy-fifth anniversary, was Denison, not far from Red River in Grayson County. The Missouri, Kansas and Texas Rail Road was primarily responsible for Denison being laid out as a town, and the residents of Sherman of that day assured the permanence and growth of the upstart settlement.

The Katy Rail Road—to use the popular name—asked Sherman for a reasonable bonus for building into the town when the road was nearing Red River. That was the custom then, and towns paid willingly, as a rule. But Sherman, or the men who were the folks who had the sayso, refused to put up. They told the Katy people, in effect, that the road would have to come to Sherman without a bonus. The Transcontinental was there, running east and west, the Houston and Texas Central was building there from the south. Naturally the Katy must have connection with those roads, so Sherman failed to ante.

But the Katy people said, in effect, that the Katy did not have to go anywhere except where its builders decided to go. The road stopped where a townsite had been laid out, and presently built branches, east and west, curving to the south, and left Sherman with two railroads instead of three.

Sherman made up for the mistake of not meeting the terms of the Katy Rail Road. Other roads were subsidized by the citizens, Austin College was brought to Sherman, and an extension of the Katy itself was made. With the advantage of being the county seat, Sherman has grown to be a city.

[237]

When the Katy was nearing the river and building its bridge into Texas, a shack town was built near the south bank of the river and named Red River City. It was hoped the Katy would make its terminus there, but some of the Katy stockholders decided a better site was further from the river. They bought a tract of land, surveyed and platted it into lots, and had the first sale of lots September 23, 1872. The first business "houses" were tents, but frame buildings soon began to take their place. The rail road bridge was completed in December, and late Christmas Day, 1872, the first passenger train rolled into Denison, giving Texas rail connection with the North and East. The train carried two coaches and a Pullman and had about a hundred passengers. Among these were the Indian chiefs, Santanta and Big Tree, convicted in Parker County, Texas, of heading a band that murdered the members of a wagon train, and on the way to the Texas penitentiary at Huntsville.

The Central Rail Road built to Red River City, but Denison was so much better in location that the people of the shack town on the river began moving to Denison. In July, 1874, the Central moved all its property from there and abandoned it as a station. The post office that had been there little more than a year was transferred to Denison and the post master of Red River City leased a lot on Denison's main street, moved his buildings from Red River City and announced he would open up with a stock of fine liquors.

He did not have the first saloon in Denison by any means. They were the first business there and for a long time supplied not only liquor but had gambling in connection, and were flanked by dance halls and bawdy houses. One street especially, named Skiddy street in honor of a Katy director, was practically nothing else for several years, and kept the police and other peace officers busy. Later the name was changed to Chestnut street.

[*238*]

One of the residents of those days, still living (1947) said there were two prosperous businesses—saloons and undertakers, an average of one undertaker to three saloons. There was plenty of heavy drinking, he said, and this led to shootings and killings. He delivered milk for his mother to a boarding house each morning and it was common to see bodies laying in the gutters—some dead, others in a drunken stupor.

When the railroad came into Denison cattlemen began driving cattle there for shipment north instead of driving them over the long trail to Kansas. This brought herd drivers, who found women and whisky plentiful and acted accordingly, keeping the officers busy. The town had policemen, and for a long time Lee Hall, the red headed nemesis of lawbreakers, was a deputy sheriff stationed in Denison after being city marshal of Sherman a short time. Sometimes they had to do with real criminals. At other times it was only a drunk attempting to terrorize the people, and being put in the city jail to become sober and next morning pay a fine.

When Denison was two years old it was honored by a visit from President U. S. Grant, in October, 1874. The President was accompanied by his wife and several Army officers, including General P. H. Sheridan. They arrived on a Sunday night and returned north next morning. General Sheridan left the train at Caddo and went across country to Fort Sill to inspect the post and plan for better protection of the frontier against Indians. It was the first visit of a United States President while in office, and had been made at solicitation of the Katy officials who realized it would be a fine advertisement for the road.

Sometimes the visitors put on exhibitions that were amusing and harmless. One was a cattleman from west Texas who sold a herd for a good price and was feeling fine. He went into a barber shop to get shaved and concluded to make a show of it, so he paid the barber $2.50 to

[239]

move his chair onto the sidewalk and shave him there in view of an admiring crowd.

Carrie Nation visited the city in 1902, and went to other cities, lecturing and selling toy hatchets. A newspaper story said she "roasted the inebriates of Sherman, Fort Worth and Austin and in several instances slapped cigars from the mouths of young men who were in her reach."

There was constructive work in and about Denison even in the early years. A cotton compress was built in 1873, the two railroads built a fine union station, the citizens built the first public free school in Texas, set aside a public park, skated in Winter on the ice on the stockyards pond under Chinese lanterns, held church festivals and attended highbrow lectures when speakers could be had.

They manufactured brick and quarried stone from near the town, and burned lime for building purposes. In 1874 Denison people supplied brick, stone, lime and sand for the Collin County court house in McKinney, which was built by a Denison contractor, besides furnishing materials for permanent buildings in Denison. There was a distributor for beer and ice, shipped from Milwaukee, and sent to Texas towns and cities down the Central. One shipment noted in a newspaper was beer for McKinney, Dallas, Ennis, Corsicana and Marlin, and 30 cases of soda pop for Corsicana.

There was other construction worthy of note. The first wagon bridge across the river was built by B. F. Colbert, a well-to-do Indian who lived north of Denison in the Territory. He had a ferry before the railroad came, which he operated until 1875, when his wagon toll bridge was completed at a cost of $40,000. It was 577 feet long and 16 feet wide, with a 24-foot turnout for passing in the middle of the bridge. It was built below the railroad bridge and on the site of the ferry. In May, 1876, there was a flood in Red River that washed out both bridges, and until the railroad bridge was rebuilt passengers and freight had to go over on a ferry to the train on the north side.

Colbert operated his ferry 22 years before he built his bridge, and a barrel set on a sled stood at the north side into which the silver dollars were pitched by people who crossed. A man who crossed in 1870 told of the barrel and said that when night came Colbert would go down and hitch a horse to the sled and haul the money to the house, or if he was indisposed he sent a Negro boy to bring in the money. Although there were other ferries near Denison, the Colbert Ferry, in 1872 brought 19,000 wagons into Texas, besides horsemen and foot travelers.

Another notable construction was the Frontier Telegraph line, built by the War Department to connect the Army posts on the frontier, and also used for private messages. Denison was headquarters because the Katy Rail Road already had a line which gave connection with the North and East. The first pole was set in Denison at the building selected for the office, November 12, 1874. The instruments were in position and the batteries were charged, and 3,500 poles had been distributed along the proposed line to Fort Richardson. Jerry Nolan, a railroad contractor who had settled in Denison after the Katy was built, contracted to get out poles which were cut about twenty miles up the river. Lieutenant Capron, in personal charge of construction, said the Negro soldiers would construct five to ten miles a day. A weather station was a part of the installation.

The line ran from Denison through Pilot Point, Denton County, then through Decatur to Jacksboro, to Fort Richardson, Fort Griffin and Concho to the Pecos, then to Forts Clark and Duncan on the Rio Grande and down the river to Brownsville, with a branch from Richardson to Fort Sill in Indian Territory. Denison and Pilot Point mayors exchanged greetings when the wire reached the latter town, in April, 1875, and Pilot Point was invited to come up and see Denison by gaslight, a company having installed a gas plant in the town. In February, 1876, the line was completed to Fort Stockton, and prairie fires were burning some of the poles while others were pushed over by buffaloes scratching themselves against the poles.

Denison had started on the way to become a city, and reached its goal.

McCurtain, Choctaw and Bryan Counties

WE MAY PRESUME that when the Federal Government forced the Indians to leave their lands and homes in the states east of the Mississippi River, and take in exchange lands across the Father of Waters, it was sincere in promising that the land should be theirs as long as grass grew and water ran. That was more than one hundred years ago, and many things can occur in a century to make changes of policy advisable, and to justify broken agreements.

That is what happened in the later years of the Nineteenth Century. White people went into Indian Territory and married Indian wives, thus becoming citizens by adoption. Some went in and remained on permits issued by the tribal authorities. Others just went in and asked no permission nor made any move to keep within the laws. It was a condition that demanded some drastic changes and steps were taken to make them.

There was nothing the Indians could do. They were not voters and so had little consideration by men who held office by favor of voters. Many of the more intelligent Indians realized that something had to be done, and they directed their efforts towards getting the best terms possible.

With congressional action providing for what became known as the Dawes Commission, which was to reach

[242]

agreements with the Five Civilized Tribes to accept individual allotments of land, give up tribal government and become a Territory, the beginning of statehood was made. It became a fact in 1907 when Indian Territory and Oklahoma Territory were combined and made the State of Oklahoma. Before that time surveys had been made by the Dawes Commission, the lands allotted and many townsites surveyed. The Convention which wrote the Oklahoma Constitution also fixed the boundaries of the counties, named them and designated the county seats, which, however, might be changed by vote of the people.

About five years before statehood for Oklahoma, a lumber company was building a rail road from Ashdown, Arkansas, into the pine lands of Eastern Indian Territory, and in 1902 it crossed the Frisco north of Paris, and ten miles north of Red River, gradually building west to Ardmore. It was then a railroad for carrying passengers and freight, and called the Arkansas and Choctaw Rail Road. Towns were established along the line, the townsites being surveyed by the Dawes Commission and approved by the Department of the Interior in Washington. The Valley then had two railroads almost paralleling Red River, and two crossing it from the north. The rail roads were largely instrumental in drawing an increase in population, and preparing the country for statehood.

MCCURTAIN COUNTY is the most eastern of the three counties in the Valley. It was named for Green McCurtain, one of the most influential of the Choctaw principal chiefs and a man of education and intelligence. A town in another part of Oklahoma is also named for him. The end of the march of the Choctaws coming from their old homes was in today's McCurtain County, and a number of mission schools and churches were established at various points in that area.

[243]

When the Arkansas and Choctaw Rail Road was built a townsite was surveyed and lots sold and buildings erected. This town was called Idabel, and was said to have been named for the daughters of two of the officials of the rail road, the two names combined to make the name of the town. Idabel was designated as the county seat for McCurtain County, and has grown to be a prosperous small city.

In the county area were old Shawneetown, for several years county seat of Miller County when Arkansas Territory had jurisdiction over that part of the Territory, and the center of the Pecan Point settlements was on the river southeast of Idabel.

In the last quarter of the Nineteenth Century, when Texas people went into the Indian Territory to shoot deer and turkeys, and to fish the swift-running streams, they usually went in groups and camped while they hunted. One of the most popular places for camping was the Sulphur Springs, which Choctaw Indians called Alikchi, now in McCurtain County. Many parties went also for the sulphur water, and families were camped there frequently during the Summer.

Alikchi was a Choctaw court ground. A small court house and jail was built there, several stores, some residences and for a time a hotel, made a sizeable village. It was at Alikchi court house that the last execution under Indian laws was carried out, when William Goings was shot by the sheriff after conviction for murder.

After the Indian courts lost their jurisdiction, and the saw mills had cut most of the merchantable pine, the village gradually faded away, and the little valley in the hills of McCurtain County resumed its original quiet.

CHOCTAW COUNTY was so named in honor of the tribe which had first made their homes there. The Arkansas and Choctaw Rail Road crossed the Frisco a few miles south of a Frisco station named Goodland, and when the rail road came, Goodland moved piecemeal to the crossing of the roads. Land east of the Frisco was owned by Joel Spring, and on the west J. J. Thomas owned a tract. Thomas built a store and in it was the first post office. Originally called Raymond, when a post office was applied for it was found that there was a post office of that name in the Territory, and the name Hugo was suggested by one of the women residents and adopted. After the east side of the railroad began to have some buildings some men went over to the west side one night and took as much of the post office equipment as they could carry over to the east side. The next day the west side people came and returned it to its original place.

There was keen rivalry between the two sides of the town. Robert Overstreet promoted the east side on the Joel Spring property, some brick houses were built, and when the Frisco abandoned its temporary depot at the rail road crossing, and built a good one several blocks north, the west side gradually deteriorated and the principal business of the town remains on the east side of the Frisco.

When the town site was surveyed anyone who had what the law called an "improvement" on a lot had first opportunity to buy the lot at the price set by the Dawes Commission which made the townsite surveys. A few pieces of lumber which might be claimed to be for the building of a house was considered an improvement, and while the survey was being made many of the lots were thus improved. The survey provided for a public square, but a man had an improvement on a part of it, others laid claim to other parts of it, so it was surveyed into lots and Hugo has no public square.

Hugo was designated county seat of Choctaw County and has the court house; has grown from a sprawling village into a well built small city. Almost in the center of Choctaw County it has on every side historic sites, which

[245]

include the grounds and burial ground of Rose Hill, palatial home of Colonel Robert M. Jones which was destroyed by fire many years ago; the Goodland Indian Orphanage and school that was established as a small mission in 1848, and began its real service two years later under the Reverend O. P. Stark; and lesser mementos of the Indians and early settlers.

BRYAN COUNTY, the western of the three Valley counties fronting Red River, has Durant for its county seat, named for the man who built the first house on the site. More than one hundred years ago a French-Canadian, Pierre DuRant (the French writing of the name) came to the Choctaw country in Mississippi, married a Choctaw woman and settled southeast of Chickasaw Bluffs which is now Memphis, Tennessee. In 1832 he and his family, which included four sons, traveled with some other families to Chickasaw Bluffs, went on a steamboat down the Mississippi, up the Arkansas to Little Rock, then overland to the eastern part of what was to be the Choctaw Nation. The sons settled in various parts of the new land. Some stayed near the Arkansas line, one went to where now is the town of Bennington, in eastern Bryan County, and another, Fisher Durant, who had married a fullblood Choctaw woman, went about twenty miles further west and built his house where is now the City of Durant.

Until the division of the lands to individuals the Indians could not sell land, though each could cultivate and control as much as he chose. When the Katy Rail Road came through the land claimed by the Durant family it had been granted right-of-way by the Federal government and the Indian Council. One of Fisher Durant's sons, whose claim was on each side of the rail road, built a store and later leased land to the people who came to the rail road and wanted to build homes and business houses. With the good

[246]

people there came others not so desirable, as in the history of all new towns. The railroad gave the name Durant Station, because of ownership of the land, and after some years dropped the "station," leaving the name the city bears today.

Durant, like Hugo in Choctaw County, was surveyed to have a public square, and like Hugo some "sooners" made "improvements" on the lots in the designated square, and as a result there is no public square in Durant. The Arkansas and Choctaw Rail Road built through to Ardmore, and this added to the growth of the town.

In addition to being in the Valley of Red River, Durant has the Washita on the west and Blue on the east, making the city what has been called "Queen of Three Valleys." It was the only Oklahoma Valley town that had its designation as the county seat contested. When an election was ordered and held, in 1908, Durant won by a clear majority over three other towns that wanted the advantages offered by a county seat.

In 1886 Peter Maytubby advertised that Caddo Springs, which he owned (as much as any Indian owned a specific piece of land), was open for visitors. He said there were eight springs, four miles west of the town of Caddo, and first-class hotel accommodation was offered. Board and room was $1.50 a day or $30 a month. There was deer, turkey, quail and prairie chicken shooting for the sportsman. On the whole it was "A quiet, healthful retreat where visitors can enjoy themselves without conventionalities of the fashionable watering places."

BURIED TREASURE

Legends of gold and silver drew many searchers but no finders.

A barrel of whisky and a walnut log were found and turned into money.

TALES OF BURIED TREASURE have been current in the Valley for years, and there have been treasure hunters who were sure they had the map or the clue that would show them exactly where the gold and silver was buried. If any was ever found it was kept secret, and there was never any evidence of any being found.

The most persistent legend, and perhaps most widely believed, was of a lot of gold bars in buckskin bags that was deposited in a lake near Red River. Before the day of the Texas Republic the Spaniards had some small garrisons at various places on Red River. The soldiers were supplied by boat when there was enough water in the river, at other times by pack trains. The route of these trains was along the south side of the river, generally not far from it.

After Mexico gained her independence from Spain these garrisons were abandoned, and traveling traders sometimes had to battle Indians from the west. Oldtimers in the Valley used to tell of a Mexican Army officer coming with crude maps of parts of the Valley, which were said to have been given him by one of the survivors of a battle with Indians, who escaped and returned to Mexico. The story was that a band of Mexican traders traveling down the river trail with a train of burros had a quantity of gold and silver bars from Mexican mines, and being attacked by Indians they threw the rawhide sacks containing the metal into a lake near the river to keep the Indians from getting it. Years later, when the land in the neighborhood of where the battle occurred was being cleared and plowed, some skeletons of men and some gun barrels were found, and this increased belief in the legend, as there had been a small lake near the place.

Even as late as some years after the beginning of the Twentieth Century, there have been treasure hunters. Some years ago a farmer who owned land on Red River

[251]

in Lamar County saw a man walking back and forth, carrying in front of him a contraption that the farmer supposed was a divining rod, as he had heard such things were to be had. The man scowled at him and said if he had no business there he had better be leaving. The farmer never knew when the man came or went.

Captain S. J. Wright owned a plantation on the river that had been owned by his father near a hundred years before. With so much hunting and hole digging going on Captain Wright concluded there might be something in the legends. He was in St. Louis on business and went to Aloe's instrument house and asked Aloe to make a treasure finder, something after the shape of the water witch that is used in locating underground water. Aloe said there was no such instrument, but if there was and they could make one it would certainly not be for sale.

There have been some discoveries of "treasure" along Red River, though they were not coins or bullion. In the 'fifties of the last century C. C. Alexander was a merchant in Paris. He had a small steamer that brought merchandise from New Orleans and carried cotton back. The steamer struck a snag near Slate Shoals northeast of Paris and sank and presently was covered with sand washed over it when the river rose. Many years later another rise washed the sand off and the boat was visible. The cargo was spoiled but one barrel was taken out that was full of whisky, as good as the day it was shipped, or better, from being "aged in the wood."

A man who found a walnut log after another washout above Arthur City floated it to a lumber mill at Arthur City to have it cut into lengths for shipping. Much black walnut was being sent to Hamburg, Germany, and brought a good price. When this log was put under the saw it was found to be "curly" walnut, and it brought the finder $1,500. Curly walnut, caused by a twist of the tree when young, was considered especially valuable.

[252]

SOME UNUSUAL INCIDENTS

"I will tell you now
What never yet was heard in tale or song."
—John Milton

Tariff Collector Was Kidnapped

COLONEL JAMES BOURLAND, native of South Carolina, came to Texas to recoup his fortunes, his business of trading and selling Negro slaves and horses and mules in Tennessee having played out. He stopped in Paris, where he found the Chisum and Wright families, from Tennessee, and was appointed a deputy surveyor for the Red River District. He was one of the men who was with General Tarrant in the Village Creek fight with Indians, and then was made by President Sam Houston collector of customs on Red River to the Louisiana line. He sometimes had trouble making collections from boats that brought merchandise, as some United States citizens had no high opinion of the struggling Republic of Texas.

A boat of which Captain Scott, an Arkansas citizen, was master, had tied up to discharge cargo, and Colonel Bourland ordered Scott to not move his boat until the duties were paid. Bourland was alone and Scott had his men tie the collector, then slipped the boat's cable and left. Bourland reported to President Houston, and it in turn was reported to Washington, and the United States finally paid Texas $26,000 for the duties and damages.

Wanted To Sell Brother's Grave Marker

IN PARIS, TEXAS, in 1884, Gustav Klein, a German, operated a business cutting tombstones. He died, and having no family one of his friends was named administrator of the estate. After funeral expenses the remainder of Klein's money was sent to his relatives in Germany. A tombstone was put over his grave by the administrator, and a picture of it was sent to the relatives so they could see Klein was properly remembered.

[255]

In 1923 Mayor J. W. De Weese of Paris received a letter, addressed to The Town Authority. It was from Oswald Klein, living in Koln, Germany, and asked if it was possible to sell the fine monument at his brother's grave and send him the money, as he was in need and thought his brother would have been forgotten after near forty years. He said, "My older brother and a sister are deceased, in the meantime and still a sister of me, having 78 years, for the livelihood of which I have in part to bear, lives in needy circumstances. After the war we remain in great sufferance and the dearness is unbounded."

A newspaper man who was shown the letter told the story in the newspaper. A monument dealer said the stone was good and could be worked over and would be worth $50 and a smaller stone. But people who read the story began sending the mayor contributions. They amounted to $58.50 and this was sent to the brother, and the stone left on the grave.

"I Am His Son"

IN 1902 Uncle Jack Roberts, an old and respected citizen living in northwest Lamar County, was found dead in bed with his throat cut. Investigation resulted in arrest of John Killian, his hired man, and Roberts' second wife, much younger than her husband. At the trial of Killian a special venire had been summoned from the jurors who had been drawn for the term of court, and as usual were being examined to determine their qualifications to serve as jurors. Among them was a man named Roberts who answered when his name was called. The prosecuting attorney asked casually if he was related to the dead man, their names being the same, and the answer was, "I am his son." He was a son of Uncle Jack's first marriage, and, of course, was excused. Killian and the woman, who was tried later, were both convicted and given penitentiary terms on circumstantial evidence.

[256]

How O. Max Gardner Got His Name

IN THE EARLY 'EIGHTIES two men came from North Carolina to Paris, Texas, Jap and June Gardner. They were half-brothers, sons of a physician who lived in the western part of the state. They engaged in trading livestock, and Jap, the older man, was shot by a horse trader with whom he had an argument near Honey Grove. He was taken to Paris and died there. June Gardner presently bought a wagon and buggy selling business from a Paris man. The house burned one night. Officers found evidence that it was set afire and June Gardner was indicted and tried on a charge of arson. Friends rallied to his defense, and his father employed the firm of Maxey, Lightfoot and Denton to defend June, who was acquitted. General Maxey was then a United States Senator, but the Congress had adjourned and he kept his connection with the firm and appeared in court when retained. After his acquittal June Gardner went back to North Carolina. His father had in the meantime married a third time, and when a son was born of that marriage he was named for General Maxey, as a mark of the father's appreciation. The son grew to manhood and in 1929 became Governor O. Max Gardner of North Carolina and served four years.

Survey Cornered on Tobacco Quid

SAMUEL BONHAM was Grayson County surveyor, then went to Austin and was employed as a surveyor for the Land Commissioner. He surveyed much of the western land belonging to the State. It was customary to start the corner of a section by noting in the field notes a nearby tree or boulder or other object that would be used in making the record of the survey. With Bonham on one of his trips was a helper who chewed large quids of tobacco. They were starting a section where there were no natural objects so a stake was driven for the first corner. The big

[257]

tobacco chewer pulled up the stake and spit his quid into the hole before replacing the stake, whereupon Surveyor Bonham wrote in his field notes the location of the section, and added, "Cornered on a chew of tobacco."

Hot Water Was Not Illegal

In 1871 G. O. Greiner, a German who had emigrated to United States, was mayor of Paris. At the same time his brother, C. F. Greiner, was mayor of Clarksville, and the latter's son, Ferdinand, was City Marshal of Clarksville. The Paris Mayor was a shoemaker, and at that time the Mayor was also judge of the police court. As there was no city hall in Paris then, he held court in his shoe shop. A woman living in the red light district was annoyed by a man visitor and failing to get rid of him she poured the contents of a kettle of hot water on him, whereupon he had her arrested for assault. The woman's lawyer argued that no assault had been committed, that the statute defined assault as beating or striking with the fists or a club or other weapon; that nowhere was there mention of throwing water; that the woman was within her right in defending her home, and that her morality, which the prosecution had brought out, was of no bearing. Mayor Greiner took down his law book, thumbed through the pages, declared there was no mention of pouring water on a person being illegal, and discharged the woman.

Collector Figured to Fraction of a Cent

The night of December 25, 1866, when the people of Paris, Texas, were celebrating Christmas, the safe in the store of Wright & Gibbons, on the public square, was broken open and robbed. The tax collector of Lamar County had no safe, and he and other people were allowed to keep money in the store safe, as there were no banks.

The entry on the minutes of the Lamar County Court relates that all the money stolen amounted to about $4,000, and that all except six or eight dollars was in currency.

The collector's books showed that he had in the safe State and county money amounting to $2,339.92 & 44/45. How the collector could have 44/45 of one cent must have been because of the discount on currency at the time, when coin was the only money with a par value. However, that is the record. The money was never recovered, nor the burglars arrested. The county and State later relieved the collector and his bondsmen by order of the court and an act of the Legislature.

He Never Had Any Fun

WHEN FEDERAL COURTS were established in the Indian Territory they were a novelty to many people and they brought out of the forks of the creeks some odd characters. One man summoned as a grand juror lived at Kemp and said the first time he ever rode on a train was when he left home to go to court. Before this, he said, he had never been in a court room, had never uttered an oath, had never used tobacco in any form, had never gambled and never danced. He was 52 years old and had lived in Chickasaw Nation 14 years, where he came from North Carolina. He added he had never tasted intoxicating liquor, had not drank tea or coffee in 30 years, had never attended a theater but had been to a barbecue 20 years before. He was a member of a church. The men who heard him tell all this decided he had "never had any fun."

Man of Good Reputation

IN ANOTHER COURT a man was on trial for assault and battery. The Government had brought a witness who testified, when questioned by the district attorney, that the man who claimed to have been assaulted was of good

[259]

character and reputation. When the defendant's attorney was told to take the witness, he asked, "Don't you know that this man who claims to have been assaulted without cause, frequently gets into trouble with his neighbors?" The witness admitted he did know that.

"Don't you know that every time he gets drunk he whips his wife, and that he was arrested last Spring for beating a boy, and that he engages in quarrels every time he goes to town?" The witness said this was also true.

"Then," said the attorney for defense, "You know all this and come before this Court and say his reputation is good in the neighborhood where he lived?" The witness said, "Oh, it takes more than that to give a man a hard reputation up where I live," and he did not seem to think that his answer was anything out of the ordinary.

Fired Engine For Casey Jones

CHARLIE DOSTER, born and reared on a Lamar County, Texas, farm, went, when 21 years old, to Oxford, Mississippi, to attend a commercial school and learn to keep books. He was at the Illinois Central depot one day when Casey Jones came through on his 638 engine, pulling a freight train from Water Valley, Mississippi, to Jackson, Tennessee. When he heard Casey's whistle, Charlie decided he was going to be a railroad engineer and not a bookkeeper. He went to Water Valley, a division point, and got on as a fireman and presently he was assigned to No. 638, where Casey taught him how to fire an engine. In due time, Doster became an engineer.

In 1899 Casey was taken off the freight and assigned to drive the Cannon Ball passenger train, from Memphis, Tennessee, to Canton, Mississippi, a 200-mile run. A Negro fireman was with Casey the night in April, 1900, when Casey died at Vaughan, just 15 miles north of the

[260]

end of his run. A freight train had a caboose, two cars of corn and a car of lumber sticking out on the main line. There was a sharp curve and from his side of the cab Casey could not see the red light on the caboose, but the Negro saw it and said, "Jump for your life, Mr. Jones, there's a caboose on the track." Casey replied, "You jump, Flim, I must stop the train." Flim jumped and was not hurt, but Casey stayed at the throttle and saved the lives of some of the 200 passengers on the train.

Doster had ended his run and gone to bed in Canton when the call boy waked him, telling him he was called to take out a wrecker. Doster raced his wrecker to Vaughan and helped take Casey out. Casey was not scalded, and one hand was on the air brake, the other hand holding his crucifix which he always wore from a small chain around his neck. Doster, long since retired, said Casey never drank, though good whisky could be had for a dollar a quart, that he was a good Catholic and lived a clean life and died a hero.

How Dead Buffalo Got Away

IN THE WINTER OF 1836 Henry Skidmore and some neighbors went up Red River prospecting on about the same trail Davy Crockett had taken when hunting buffalo. The weather changed suddenly and a heavy snowfall added to their discomfort. Provisions were running low when one of the party killed a buffalo, but while they were skinning the animal, it got away. When Henry told this story he waited a moment for someone to ask how a dead buffalo could get away. Then he would tell them that they had the skin off one side, turned the animal over, it was near the sloping bank of the river which was covered with snow. The buffalo slipped down the bank into the icy water and could not be gotten out.

[*261*]

Flood "Totally Destroyed" His Farm

AFTER THE RED RIVER FLOOD OF 1908 a landowner brought suit against the Frisco Rail Road, claiming that work done by the rail road to prevent damage to its bridge at Arthur City had caused the overflow on his farm and ruined his valuable land. He sued for $6,000 and the jury that heard the case gave him a verdict for $3,000. His entire property, real and personal, was on the tax rolls for $800, but the Court refused to let this be shown to the jury. It was said that after the trial a juror told a friend that they gave the man $3,000 because they believed he needed the money, and that his land had really been damaged to some extent. After a lesser flood some years later, the same farmer went to his lawyer and asked him to file another suit. The lawyer dissuaded him by recalling that at the former trial the owner had testified that his farm was "totally" destroyed.

Two Notable "Firsts"

TWO "FIRSTS" are a part of the Valley, though by no means connected. One was the visit to Paris by Miss Frances Willard, who came at the invitation of Captain E. L. Dohoney and lectured in the early 'eighties. Following her visit the first Woman's Christian Temperance Union in Texas was organized. Mrs. A. P. Boyd, a Paris woman, was the first editor of the "White Ribbon," the official publication of the Union in Texas.

The first Coca-Cola that came to the Valley was received and dispensed from his fountain by Frank Ledger, a Paris confectioner. It was a one-gallon jug, shipped on trial by an Atlanta, Georgia drug house. M. P. Alexander, who was employed by the druggists, and who later made his home in Paris, said he realized the value of the mixture as a fountain drink, and induced his employers to let him send out some samples, which was done. Before that time it had been sold only in Atlanta.

IN LIGHTER VEIN

*"What an ornament and safeguard
is humor . . . It is a genius itself,
and so defends from the inanities."*
—*Sir Walter Scott*

NOT EVERYTHING in the Valley was tragedy and law-lessness. There was comedy of a sort at times, and people laughed perhaps as much as they wept or "viewed with alarm." One of the early providers of mirth was a good citizen, Hiram Duff, whose friends shortened the name to Hi. He was jovial in disposition and when he laughed it was not only apparent to bystanders that he was amused but people at some distance were made aware of it.

In the Summer of 1843 Lamar County court was held at Mount Vernon, several miles south of where now is Paris. Mount Vernon had been selected by vote of the people as being about the geographical center of the coun-ty, but no court house was built on the tract donated to the county by Matt Click. Court was held in Click's tavern, but it was hot, so the court moved to a large bois d'arc tree near the house. Hi Duff rode by and seeing the assembly asked what was doing. Being told that court was sitting he was amused. Seeing a court out of doors was something new and he gave voice to his amusement in his usual man-ner. So loud was his laughter, in fact, that the Court ordered the sheriff to arrest Mr. Duff and bring him before the Court for contempt. That was easier said than done, for Hi had no desire to be fined, so he put spurs to his horse and headed across the prairie. The sheriff rode after him, but the records of that court have been destroyed and whether he was caught or fined is not known.

Some years afterwards Mr. Duff bought a 200-acre farm in the country northeast of Paris and settled down to a farmer's life. In Paris one day he saw a fine pair of spurs a smith had made, and he asked to buy them. The smith was not anxious to sell and finally Hi told him he would give him a good substantial horse in exchange for the spurs. The smith agreed and was told he would have to go to Hi's farm to get the horse. So the smith went out

[265]

when it was convenient. Hi was not at home and his wife told the smith he had ridden off and she did not know when he would return. The smith told her he had come to get the horse Hi had traded him and Mrs. Duff said so far as she knew Hi had but one horse which he rode when he left the house. The smith said Hi had told him he would find the horse in the yard, and Mrs. Duff said the only horse in the yard was a saddle maker's horse, the wooden vise which leather workers used to hold their work while sewing. The smith decided he had been outwitted and departed. Hi had used it to hold a piece of hickory when he shaved a wagon spoke or an axe handle, and it was just what he had represented it to be in his trade with the smith, "a good, substantial horse."

Abner Neathery was one of the early arrivals in the Valley and settled in southern Lamar County near Matt Click's tavern. He married Matt's daughter, Louisa, and one Sunday morning suggested to her that they attend preaching as there was to be service a few miles from their home. So while Louisa prepared for church, Abner went out to catch a couple of horses. He found one for himself and looking for one for Louisa came in sight of the still house on the creek and dropped in for a nip. Swapping yarns with the boys there he forgot about his wife and rode on to the preaching, and took part in the singing. About the time the preacher's two-hour sermon ended Louisa came in. She had walked to the preaching and was hot and "put out." Abner, hoping to mollify her, asked the preacher if he couldn't preach another sermon for Louisa, who had come all the way to hear him, but the preacher said he did not feel equal to that, so Abner said maybe a hymn would do. Thereupon the good man lined out another hymn, Abner joined in with vigor, and Louisa had to be content with that.

Abner rode out once with some neighbors when he was living in Hopkins County, where Indians raided oftener

[266]

than in Lamar. One day there was report of Indians being in the neighborhood and the men had gone out to try to kill or drive them off. They rode several miles and seeing no Indian sign decided to get back home. They stopped at a creek to water the horses and rest a while and were lying around in the shade when one of the party saw something he mistook for Indians on the horizon and gave the alarm. The men scrambled up and caught their horses that were grazing while the riders rested, and began a retreat, for they were under the impression that the Indians were in force too big for them to tackle. Abner was slow in getting mounted, his horse being further off, and he was behind, when one of the others looked back and called to him to hurry else the Indians would get him. Abner, doing his best to get his old nag into a gallop, replied, "Hurry the dickens. You don't reckon I'm riding jockey in a case like this, do you?" He never lacked for repartee.

John Boyd, a blacksmith and farmer was a good citizen and one of those rugged individualists who started Texas on the right road. He came to Paris one day from his farm and having attended to business he walked around to see what was going on. Court was in session on the second floor of the house in the center of the public square and Mr. Boyd went up. Seeing some friends he did not meet every day he walked around shaking hands and conversing. He had on a pair of new and squeaky boots, and the noise disturbed the judge who told Mr. Boyd to sit down. He did so, but not for long and his boots again disturbed the Court, who told him he was fined $10 for contempt. Mr. Boyd walked up to the clerk's desk, laid down a gold piece and said, "I'm a horse." The judge thereupon told Sheriff John Bland to take Mr. Boyd to jail and lock him up until he was sober.

Mr. Boyd made no resistance and they went to the jail a block and a half from the court house, but when the sheriff opened a cell door and told Mr. Boyd to enter the latter looked in, then drew back and said under no manner of means would he go in there, that there was something in there he was afraid of. Thinking to humor him the sheriff stepped in the cell to show there was nothing, and Mr. Boyd shut the cell door, locked it, took the key and departed. He went back to the courthouse and sat down. Presently the sheriff was needed to call a witness but the sheriff was absent. After he was hunted for, Mr. Boyd said, "I can tell you where Sheriff Bland is," and told what he had done. The judge told him that if the key was not given up at once he would be fined $100, so he handed the key to a deputy who by this time had appeared, and walked out of the courtroom. The room was reached by stairs outside the house, and Mr. Boyd stopped on the platform at the head of the stairs, turned and called to the judge, "You can go to hell with your nigger court," and walked down the stairs.

This was in reconstruction days in the years after the war between the sections, when Negroes were put on juries. Like many others Mr. Boyd did not like that, and it accounted in part at least for his actions. The sheriff was released and court continued its business.

C. D. Purdon was a civil engineer, born in Ireland, who was employed by the St. Louis & San Francisco Rail Road Company to survey its line through Choctaw Nation, and build a bridge over Red River north of Paris. While engaged in this work he had his first contact with Choctaw Indians, and in his diary he noted some humorous things.

Some contractors were brought horseback along the proposed line of the railroad so they could get an idea of the work they were to bid on. They were all large men, and for some time afterwards the Choctaws dated from "the time them fat fellows came through."

Arriving at a settlement where he was to get a guide for further preliminary survey, Purdon asked for the man but no one had ever heard of him. When the others of his party came up, Purdon introduced himself to the storekeeper, who was a squaw man (married to an Indian woman) and the man he wanted was found in a few minutes. The Indians had thought Purdon was a deputy marshal.

The Indian guide regretted very much that a deer Purdon had wounded, while they took time out to kill some game, had been able to get away. He said he was sure that deer had a madstone in it. Then he told Purdon that if one went on a prairie where were no stones, dug a hole and buried a small stone in it, he could come back in six months and find two stones in the hole—said he "knew it for a fact."

Captain Sam Wright, a Red River plantation owner who had promoted bringing the Frisco to Paris, believed there was coal in the Valley, so he and a friend started out with two Indians, one of whom could not speak English, but knew where there was coal, according to the other Indian, who could speak English. After they had ridden several miles the two Indians began talking and the interpreter said, "He wants to know what it looks like." "What what looks like?" asked Captain Wright. "That thing you are looking for," said the interpreter. "He wants to know what it looks like so he will know it when he sees it." Captain Wright and his friend decided to quit the search.

An engineer who made part of the survey was moving camp and was warned by an Indian against the Indians further west. The engineer was using oxen to move, as they lived on the grass. This Indian told him, "Those Indians out there bad; steal all your goddams." He had heard the word used toward the oxen so much that he thought that was the name for them.

The company building the bridge had some hydraulic jacks in which alcohol was used to keep from freezing. Indians found that out and drank the alcohol. Then the bridge men put in a mixture of alcohol and coal oil, but it

[269]

went the same way. They would drink lemon extract, and any liniment that had alcohol in it.

Arthur City became a base of supply for whisky in Indian Territory, Purdon said. It came by express in various sized packages. The method was for the Territory customer to ask the express agent if there was a C. O. D. package for him for so many dollars. The amount he mentioned decided the size of the package handed to him, and his name and address was written on it after the price and express charges had been paid.

Soon after Hugo, Oklahoma, became a town, a game of baseball was played between Hugo and Antlers. The Hugo second baseman was "spiked" by the Antlers player trying to make the base, and was unable to play. So that the game would not stop, U. S. Marshal Clark Wasson, who had played ball when younger, went out to second base with his six-shooter still hanging on his belt and said the game would proceed while he covered the bag. He did and it did.

An old Choctaw talking to a friend about the automobile was reported as saying: "My boy, he take his grunt an' snort buggy out of stable in hurry an' run clear to town on big sidewalk, 30 mile long. Come back quick an' say make 60 mile hour. Well, how you fix it? If 30 mile to town an' he make 60 mile in hour, look like he get back half hour 'fore he start.

"He say, save lots time. Huh. What he do with time if he save it? Just run like helifax some other town. Maybe kill dog, or chicken, or little girl in road. Don't care—much. Also an' likewise, maybeso, some time he lose road an' can't find it while he run so quick. Then kill tire, or tree, or gully, or bridge gits in way an' he kill bridge an' car an' self. No good when dead. Worse good when crippled."

[270]

SIX MONTHS JOURNEY
TO REACH THE VALLEY

*"It cannot be too often repeated,
that it is not helps, but obstacles,
not facilities, but difficulties that
make men."*
—William Mathews

How One Family Came to the Valley

THE RIVER WAS THE MEANS by which the first Anglo-Saxons came to the Red River Valley. Trappers and traders came in canoes or dugouts before the time covered by these stories, and seldom stayed in one place long. It was in 1816 that the first complete family arrived and settled at Pecan Point, a name that was for a time used to describe all the adjacent area.

The family was that of Claiborne Wright, a Tennessean, who built and loaded a keel boat at Carthage, Tennessee, March 5, 1816, went aboard with his family, and six months later landed at Pecan Point on the north side of Red River, some miles below the mouth of the Kiamichi River. One of his sons, George W. Wright, then lacking three months of being seven years old, wrote this account of the journey in his later years. He said:

"The first boat that passed through the rafts on Red River carried a moving family under the care of Claiborne Wright in 1816. They were in an old keel boat bound for Pecan Point. At Natchitoches an Indian pilot was procured of the Pascagoula tribe and they set out about May 15 to probe their way through a dark and dismal and interminable swamp and overflow. All was dark and dreary, not a trace to be seen of civilization of any kind, nothing but a continued field of overflowed swamp, nothing in the shape of inhabitants but mosquitoes and alligators—all was dismal, nothing to be heard but the hum of the mosquitoes and the bellowing of the alligators.

"The boat arrived at the first raft, which was at the mouth of what is called the Coushatta chute, at that time a small narrow bayou overhung with swamp willows covered with long moss that reached from the topmost branches to the water and in many places you could not

[273]

see a hundred yards in midday, all was so thick. The body of the first raft was about a quarter of a mile in length and seemed to be solid as there were cottonwood trees growing on the bed of this raft at least a foot thick. The boat was weak-handed—five men and one little boy about 14 years old and a Negro woman was the strength of the crew for this wonderful undertaking. The pilot told them that the boat had to pass this mat of drifted timber. The complicated engineering work was begun and in about five days the boat was through and in open water. What rejoicing was there among the crew.

"We passed up the chute into a large inland sea or lake —one continued sheet of water as far as the eye could reach, not a star to guide the mariner on his course. All seemed lost, forever lost, so far as human observation could see, but nothing daunted the old man who had started to pass through and to make a settlement at Pecan Point pressed on and the second or third day came in sight of land. What joy to think we were almost through the difficulties, but not so, for we had fairly entered into them as it afterward proved. But the boat stopped one day and rested at the land and all hands went out to hunt and killed several deer and cut a good many trees and filled with honey all the vessels that we had that would contain it. All was well, so we cut cable and passed on up a narrow stream, called Bee bayou, about ten days, and in many places timber had to be cut to admit of the boat passing through.

"Almost all the way in this part of the overflowed river no land was to be seen but in many places we could see the tops of the rushes as they projected out of the water a few inches on what seemed to be the highest ridges as we could see them only at intervals. We finally reached another immense body of water but no land, so we passed into this immense lake and finally crossed it and found land to the great joy of all on board. Here we hunted and fished two

[274]

days, then left and passed into a narrow bayou where the undergrowth was so high at the entrance that we were detained for some time cutting the brush to enable us to enter the bayou.

"We finally passed into the channel and found a great deal of fallen timber to be cut out of the way to let the boat pass. We pressed on through difficulties of every kind that it is possible for the imagination of man to conceive for the space of three months, and finally arrived in sight of open river above what is known as the head of Willow chute. Here was the hardest point to make, for the current had drifted timber far above the banks of the river and I think the body of timber was at least 10 feet higher than the water in many places. As well as I can recollect in about 10 days the boat floated in the main channel of the river above the raft. All was joy and here we spent several days to rest and wash as the washing had not been done for several weeks.

"To look back and just imagine all the meandering that had been made and it did really seem to be impossible to have made all those turns and have gotten safely through and back into the river again. It was one continuous chain of bayous and lakes from the time we left the river at Coushatta chute until we passed out of the last, Willow chute, into the main river. There was one lake that I recollect especially, where all the wild fowl of every kind seemed to have congregated to raise their young. The lake was skirted on the north by an immense thicket, so dense that the fowls could build almost in one solid bed of nest, and really I thought the alligators had become so thick that the boat could scarcely pass through them. It seemed as though the alligators had congregated there to feast upon the young fowls as they would occasionally tumble out of their nests and an alligator would seize and devour it. I think that we got at least a barrel of eggs at that place.

"We left the head of Willow chute and passed up the

[275]

Red River for several days. Then reached the Coushatta village and they seemed quite friendly at first but when we commenced to leave they seized the cable of the boat and tied her fast and came in and helped themselves to what they wanted. That was later found a tolerably hard case, after having passed through so much hardship and toil, but it could not be helped and we had to submit. After they had taken what they wanted they offered to pay for all but had nothing to pay with that would have been of use to us.

"So we left that place and passed on for several days and came to Long Prairie. At Long Prairie we found the first settlement of whites, an old man by the name of Berry lived there and a man by the name of Morris May, and I believe that they constituted the settlement. Spent several days there and passed on to the Delaware village. It was about where Lost Prairie is, I think, but on the north bank of Red River. Buffalo were plenty all along the river in all the prairies. We passed on but there was no settlement that I can recollect until we reached Pecan Point where there was an Indian trader and some two or three white families just arrived in the country, but had raised no corn.

"Here was the long-sought home of the family, amidst a band of Indians, the only companions, and the family had never seen any except those at the Coushatta village who had robbed the boat of all they could find that they wanted. This was enough to prejudice the minds of all against the Indians. The family consisted of two old folks, two daughters and five sons, and a Negro girl and child, in the wilderness, without a house, without a horse, cow, hog or chickens and no money to get it with, no corn, no meat, only wild meat. The gun was the meat, bread, salt, coffee, house, fence—in fact, the gun was all in all, the protection, and she was considered all, for without her there could not have been anything done, for in fact everything depended upon the gun. I think I have seen as many as five deer shot

[276]

down and slain in the yard in one morning. That will give you a better idea of the wilderness of the country than anything else I could say.

"If a buffalo was wanted it could always be killed and delivered at the camp or house the same day, and if we needed fat meat all that we had to do was to call Captain Burkham's dogs and we would kill a fine bear at any time to season the lean meats. With the skins off the game that gave meat we could get an abundant supply of coffee and we could go to the woods and find and cut a bee tree and get enough honey to answer for sweetening for the family.

"All this looked strange, for the family had come from Carthage, Tennessee, where society was good and where everything could be had in the shape of comforts or luxuries. The bare idea of a family living without bread or salt was something unheard of. Provision enough to last two years had been loaded on the boat but all the flour had been on the water so long it was so badly spoiled it had to be thrown away for it made all sick—it tasted and smelled just like the musk that comes from the alligator.

"The second year after arrival of the family at this place the old man heard that a man by the name of Price had raised some corn near the Sabine landing on Little river, about 150 miles off, so he took one of his sons and borrowed two horses and went there and was able to get five bushels of corn, two bushels of which was headed up in a barrel for seed and the balance was given to the old lady and daughters to make a little nourishment for them when sick until we could raise corn—and thus things went on from time to time in that day.

"Reader, if you had to raise a family under such circumstances I fear you would complain, yet I do not recollect to have heard a murmur out of one of the family, but all seemed determined to bear all and do the best that could be done under the circumstances, for in a few days after the family landed the boat sank and that placed it

[277]

out of the power of moving from that place until sufficient means had been made to enable them to move, and by that time all seemed to be as well satisfied as though they had had an abundance of every kind of the luxuries of life and lived in palaces instead of the little hut, for the house was made of poles that one man could carry on his shoulder, so you can have some idea of the kind of house it was that the family had to occupy.

"Those were a few of the difficulties that had to be encountered to secure this fair country of which we are so proud, and yet I cannot tell the half of what had to be borne, for a great many suffered much more than did this family. Now I would ask you, how would you like to have to go through the half of what I have stated? Yet you complain at your several lots at the present, when there is everything that could have been asked for at that day. Just reflect for one moment and I think that your complaints will be hushed into perfect contentment, for I assure you that from circumstances this family seemed to me to have been peculiarly fortunate, and as for myself, I feel thankful that my lot was as good as it was."

TWO THOUSAND COPIES OF THIS BOOK

WERE PRODUCED AT EL PASO, TEXAS

Typography and Design by CARL HERTZOG

Illustrations by JOSE CISNEROS

Silhouette by JACK ELLIS

Type: Baskerville Roman

Titles and Initials: Eden

Paper: Warren's Oldstyle

Cloth: Interlaken Sactext